*To Sarah who was taken from us far too young,*

*and to Lissie for her support and patience.*

First published 2021 by Olly Sanders

Printed in the United Kingdom

ISBN 978-1-80049-981-2
The Journey, Not The Destination

Rock and Sea Adventures
Brynrefail, Caernarfon LL55 3NT
www.rockandseadventures.co.uk

# Contributors

Thanks must go to the following people.

Catrin Thomas, Sean Nugent, Paul Jeffery, Joe Simpson and Jackie Bishop for proofreading and suggestions. George Manley, Martin Doyle, Twid Turner, Stu Mcleese, Dan Jones, Ben Lawes, Simon Burke, Leo Hoare, Dave Rudkin, Lee Roberts, Karl Midlane and Liam Fleming for Photos. Thanks also to the following adventurers; Tim Niel, Martin Chester, Sid Sinfield, Nige Robinson, Roger Chandler, Nick Bullock, Sean Nugent, Iain Peter and any others I may have missed.

Special Thanks to George Manley for his fantastic drawings and Mark Anderson for putting the book together.

Thanks to The Arctic Club, BMC, Alpine club, MEF, Welsh Sports Association and The Winston Churchill memorial trust fund for funding over the years.

Plus thanks to Palm Equipment, Werner Paddles, P&H Sea Kayaks, DMM and Mountain Equipment for providing kit.

# Foreword

We have never needed explorers and adventurers more than today. The exploration mindset is one of ambitious goal setting, the joy of movement, a sense of action, the acceptance and even welcoming of tough times, the clarity of personal responsibilities and the undeniable feeling that this must be the way to live. And it's exactly that attitude that helps to build a resilient society ready to act on global issues.

The COVID-19 pandemic, caused by our out-of-balance relationship with nature, has sharpened our focus on the value of nature. Thanks to science we now have vaccines, but the only true vaccine against future pandemics is to protect nature and the way to do that is:

1. Protect what we have

2. Restore what has been damaged

3. Reset our values so that it doesn't happen again

We know this because the beautiful combination of exploration, science and adventure has produced unquestionable results from long-term data sets often produced in hostile conditions over many years. The dedicated science and support teams 'ground truthing' the planet for this information have never been more valued and their field work results are directly driving global economies and smart political decision making.

If we encourage society to be bursting with adventurous people using exploration and adventure as their compass heading, we can find solutions to the world's most pressing problems. We only need to feel the spirit in these stories from Olly to know that's true.

## PAUL **ROSE**
Explorer, TV Presenter, Public Speaker, Polar Guide & Expedition Leader and former Vice President of RGS

# Maps

PATAGONIA

ALASKA

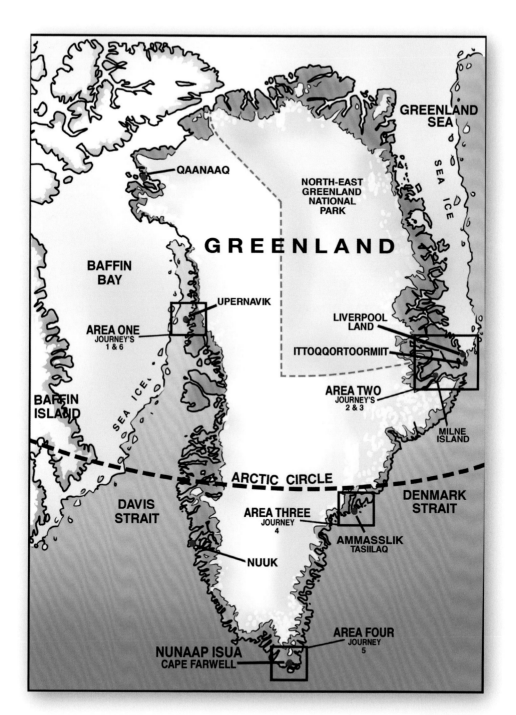

GREENLAND SEA

GREENLAND

QAANAAQ

NORTH-EAST GREENLAND NATIONAL PARK

BAFFIN BAY

UPERNAVIK

AREA ONE
JOURNEY'S
1 & 6

LIVERPOOL LAND

ITTOQQORTOORMIIT

BAFFIN ISLAND

SEA ICE

AREA TWO
JOURNEY'S
2 & 3

MILNE ISLAND

ARCTIC CIRCLE

DAVIS STRAIT

DENMARK STRAIT

AREA THREE
JOURNEY
4

AMMASSLIK
TASIILAQ

NUUK

AREA FOUR
JOURNEY
5

NUNAAP ISUA
CAPE FARWELL

**GREENLAND**

# Contents

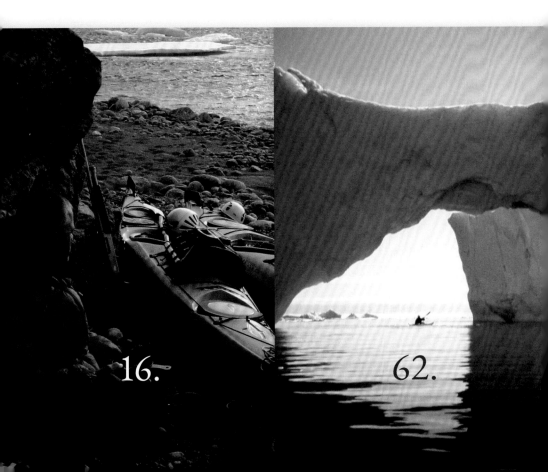

16.

62.

86.

112.

# INTRODUCTION

# "This is a collection of stories, adventures on the sea,

mountains and some life adventures. It's not deeply philosophical tales of superhuman efforts against adversity, just a set of stories about fun and friendship in wild and remote places. About when we can leave all the trappings of civilisation behind and enjoy scenery, wildlife and sitting around campfires telling stories with our mates.

I come from an era predating mobiles and social media and on most of the trips have tried to avoid having a means of contact, and savoured the time away from all that. It's not for everyone and some say foolhardy, but I think you come back truly refreshed relying on your instincts and team strengths and the confirmation, that you have visited a truly wild place and immersed yourself.

Adventure is out there in many forms, it doesn't have to be a major expedition to a remote place. It can be on your doorstep . But if you do want an expedition experience , then its not as hard as it seems. Start the process, find the right people and an idea can spring into life. All it takes is your time and commitment to see it through. I can guarantee whatever the outcome, it will be a life changing experience.

Embrace the time away from your phone and social media, don't get frustrated by problems you come across and embrace the change and flow of the journey. It will build in resilience to call on in the future and realise that things we thought as important are trappings of modern life that are sometimes constraining us and holding us back.

Most of all enjoy times with friends, tell stories and laugh a lot.

The book has taken a while to come about, the confidence in writing it down on paper and putting it out there for people to judge. I hope the reader enjoys them and I had a lot of pleasure reliving memories of the past, one of the things that cannot be taken away from us as we get older.

I would like to thank all my fellow adventurers who were part of that journey for their skill, patience, company and most of all for their humour.

**Olly Sanders**
**North Wales February 2021**

# CHAPTER ONE

# THE BEAR NECESSITIES

SIMON LOOKING NORTH FROM
RATHBONE ISLAND

# "It's above 71 degrees north on the N.E. coast of Greenland,

its July on the second day of a month's long unsupported expedition in kayaks heading north.

Simon and I are sleeping through a storm having moved the tent in the night, to get out of the full strength of the wind. I hear a noise and feel a presence; I look up, and at the end of my sleeping bag, there's the head of a polar bear! No real panic - just surprise. It had ripped into the tent to get at some food bits. What a schoolboy error!

The time seemed to unfold slowly. I shook Simon awake, lifted the pump-action shotgun from between the sleeping bags and banged the bear on the nose. I shouted - slowly it withdrew from the torn entrance of the tent. We scrambled out, to see the bear heading off with two cubs in tow.

I looked at Simon, thinking that he hadn't signed up for quite this much adventure by the sec-ond day. He was an old climbing friend who had come on board at the last moment.

We were having a day out with his wife Trys and their kids, and I had been talking about the trip; he had made a throwaway comment on how exciting it would be. So I asked straight back if he wanted to come. He hesitated, and I told him I needed to know by the following day. I rang him in the morning, told him I had funding for the trip, and he said yes, so straight away I booked all the tickets and rang him back, so now he was committed.

The idea was to explore the remote area of Liverpool Land by sea kayak and attempt new al-pine climbs we found on the way. I had funding from the Arctic Club and could use the kayaks I had left in Ittoqqortoormiit from a previous trip.

It's a very remote area, with this being the only settlement for thousands of kilometres. Further North are a few isolated research stations, and the area is patrolled by the famous Sirius dog patrol - an elite unit of Danish officers who patrol the North in winter. The main settlement is about 500 people - a mix of Danes and Inuit, and our local contact was Martin, an ex Sirius pa-trol member I knew from before, a reserved man of few words. We arrived on the last leg by helicopter and spent a day unpacking our barrels, which were shipped a few months earlier. We bought a gun off Martin and located our sea kayaks, packed them with 23 days' food, tent, tent and climbing and camping gear - it was a tight fit.

Ittoqqortoomitt is located at the mouth of Scoursbysund, the most extensive fjord system in the world. I had already done a similar trip seven years previously in the Fjord, again climbing and kayaking, with two friends Ben and Dan. A great trip, but we ran out of food towards the end and could only afford a drop-off and had to paddle back in deteriorating weather. But we had managed to climb a new significant mountain route and had encounters with narwals and musk ox.

This time, however, we were going out on the open ocean - to Martin's surprise. He reminded us we would be exposed to swell and a committing coast, due to the fact there were no acces-sible landing spots. Last time we were in the area we had come back safely from a trip much to his surprise, I think. So this time he stopped talking and simply shrugged and we set off early the next morning.

After the bear incident, we pulled the kayaks next to the tent, placing an empty whisky bottle on top of one of the kayaks. Yes, I know it was only the third day of the trip, but on other trips, we drink the bottle of whisky in the first few days, to break the ice with the team and then we don't have to worry about rationing it, but have a decent night drinking it.

Anyway, four hours later I hear the bottle go, stick my nose out of the tent to find the three bears caught like naughty schoolboys about to get stuck into the food in the kayaks. Simon and I get out of the tent and shout, and the bears slowly move on; unfortunately, the large female has the large rear hatch cover of the kayak still in her mouth.

We now chase the bears across a stream until I realise that Simon doesn't have the gun; at this moment, he also notices that I am empty-handed as well. 'You amuse them while I get the gun,' he says, sprinting back to the tent before I can argue. Luckily, by this point, the bear has spat out the somewhat unappetising plastic cover, and I quickly retrieved it and dashed back to the tent.

The wait for the storm to end is somewhat tense, waiting for the bears to return. Luckily, in the Arctic summer, there are almost 24 hours of daylight, so as soon as it calms down, we load the boats, and we're off.

**THE SECOND BEAR ENCOUNTER
ON RATHBONE ISLAND**

The sea kayak was initially designed by the Inuit as a hunting vehicle for seal, and other prey; different areas had different designs - although the new sea boats reflect these designs, the addition of rudders and watertight hatches makes life a little easier. The Inuit boats designed to fit the individual generally and made from materials available: sealskin, bone and wood. Also, swimming out of your kayak meant a likely death in the waters, so they developed elaborate skills to roll the boat while remaining in it.

Our kayaks were about 5m in length with three watertight compartments and made of plastic. With all the gear, it meant a tight fit, including the cockpit area; we had all the area in which we sat filled up and the gun strapped to the back deck in a waterproof bag. We were self-sufficient, we could go where the weather allowed and explore and move on, in a traditional craft, and climb and explore the mountains. I loved this concept and had made a few trips in this style.

Back up was an EPIRB or locator beacon with a distress button. I've always resisted the idea of a Sat phone as long as the others I'm with are happy with this. The notion of expeditions for me is to get away from all the trappings of ordinary life, engaging with the environment and the team. I also come from a generation pre-mobile and social media, and although I have embraced the technology in everyday life, expeditions for me are like a detox.

It's often hard to explain this to others, who see it as naïve and foolhardy. But we make deci-sions based on not that we have a Sat phone, but that we don't; we have to be in tune with the environment and make the right decisions, and, with most of these remote environments, in any significant trauma a Sat phone will make little difference. It's a personal decision, but I al-ways feel that the trip feels like an adventure and has an entirely different feel without a get-out-of-jail card.

The weather improved, and we headed North along the coast until we reached a large bay. This

large area contained some islands, and we intended to try and climb here.

We found an old hunter's hut on a peninsula, used in the winter when the sea is frozen, and it was a bit more reassuring to have a wooden door shut for the night rather than tent fabric.

We landed on Raffles Island and went exploring. We found some possible climbing potential on a massive cliff above a frozen lake, and the next morning we headed in. It's hard to tell the quality of the rock and the climbing till you get on it; you can pick out lines of weakness which we headed up.

We were climbing in an Alpine-style - a standard climbing rack, two 50m ropes and rock boots. The climbing was ok, but the rock was loose and scary, and we pushed on till just before the summit, where it was getting worse. From here we could traverse into a snowy gully. It was adventure climbing miles from anywhere with no backups; we'd had enough of this dangerous route.

Unfortunately, we were now in a snow gully with no crampons, and we had to rig some exciting

abseils of snow bollards to get down, the crampons being back at the tent. We got back to the shelter late that evening and watched the sun dip over the horizon and then re-emerge, bathing us in an orange glow.

Cape Hoeg has a research hut used to observe the little auks that breed in the area; a few re-mained, but the rest had gone along with the scientist as the season was coming to an end. As we opened the outer door, the door into the hut a sign above it read - 'Welcome to the Land of Passion and Luxury!'. What awaited, however, was neither - although the cabin was a welcome break from the tent, with a couple of rooms and a kerosene heater and table and chairs, most welcome.

The little auks had nested in the scree, and I had never really seen one before, and the arctic fox that provided us with some local entertainment looked well-fed from the bounty of the breed-ing season. We spent some time here mountaineering on the stunning ridges nearby, and we were able to get valuable views of further North, and the spectacular mountain scenery of the mountains of

**REPAIRING THE ROOF AT CAPE HOEG AFTER BLOWING
A HOLE IN IT BY ACCIDENT**

Liverpool Land, a look only really being possible from the ridge.

While in the hut that evening, I was checking the sequence of cartridges in the pump-action shotgun, and it went off, the solid lead slug blowing a hole in the roof. When the smell and the noise had died down, Simon looked at me in disbelief - I was supposed to be the gun expert. I had to get on the roof and repair the hole - for some reason I kept giggling, what a prick I was.

The passage further North looked blocked by sea ice, so we decided to explore the local area and headed off to Rathbone island. Our arctic fox came out to say goodbye, and we watched him get smaller as we paddled away.

We landed on the south side and found an old hut in disarray with its door off. I left Simon to get a brew on while I went in search of firewood.leaving the gun with him. I had an armful of driftwood when I saw something emerging from the water 100m away. It soon became evident that this was another bloody bear, and it was heading straight for me. I felt no real fear, just fascination. I watched it

come closer, it hadn't noticed me, but at about 50m away it got a proper smell of me and turned and legged it back into the sea and swam off.

I had surprised it, I was a smell it wasn't familiar with and luckily for me didn't like. We had come to the islands to avoid the bears - a strategy that wasn't paying off. I think it hit home when we were in the hut after a temporary repair on the door; I slept in the corner with the gun next to me.We carried the gun as a last resort , when you realise your no longer top of the food chain , but the hunted. If you go into these areas you have to be prepared to protect yourself .If not there are plenty of other adventurous areas where you wont have to make those decisions

We had been out for about 18 days, seen no one and had good weather - as we had no access to a weather report we'd had to rely on our observations and a barometer. The temperature started to drop, and the direction and size of the swell changed. We decided to head back to the safety of the fjord system, although this was a reasonable distance; but as we had endless day-light, we went for it and

**LOOKING AT RATHBONE ISLAND FROM RAFFLES ISLAND**

just kept going.

The swell picked up, and I caught occasional glimpses of Simon between the sets, his kayak al-most being airborne sometimes, before the bow crashed down in the next set. Swimming here would be bad news indeed, and we just kept going with the occasional pee stop. It was now getting colder, with sleet arriving and a darkening sky.

We came back into the entrance of the fjord system and camped on the peninsula. We didn't want to go back to civilisation just yet, we were having a good time. We got used to a relaxed and comfortable relationship that had resulted in an adventurous and safe trip with all the ex-citing parts.

When I reflect on this trip, it was committing, we had been out on the open coast with no real back up, but with many lucky breaks, some of it sounds shambolic and naïve. Still, we had both been working in the outdoors for many years, and I like to think the decisions we had control over,

were good ones.

We had sat around campfires, talked, shared experiences, laughed a lot and had time to absorb a fantastic landscape away from all the pressures of modern life.

We went back to the settlement, and the storm arrived. Winter seemed to have set in, and we had to wait for this to abate before the helicopter could fly. The once-a-month village dance event solved this problem of having to hang around.

An all-night drinking festival with dodgy music and the worst toilet in the world. The dance floor had a step up to the so-called bar, which was a stack of beer cans. No matter how pissed the locals were - and they get drunk very quickly - nobody fell over the step. I had experienced the very affectionate state the Inuit women get into after a few drinks, and Simon and I ended up dancing with the locals, Simon in his element, with happy smiling women, dancing like his dad.

# CHAPTER
## TWO

# ROCK 'N' ROLL

# "I had a good childhood.

I lived in middle England and was well looked after. My dad was a photographer and journalist, my mother was a housewife. I went to a private Catholic boy's school, although it wasn't quite like Tom Brown's Schooldays. I got beaten regularly, but we had a transparent system. It did me no harm, and you always knew there were consequences to actions, even if they seemed unfair at the time. It was good preparation for later life. Academically, I didn't shine, and I scraped through with a few O levels. Not enough for University and to be honest, I couldn't be arsed with that. So, like Dick Turpin, I headed for London with no real idea other than an offer of work from my Indian uncle in the rag trade. He had a shop on King's Road in Chelsea and was the boss. We ran around in a beat-up old transit van delivering bleached denim to other shops or working in the king's road shop.

I got some digs in Lewisham, with Paul and Dave - people I knew vaguely. Paul worked in the

29

city, and I shared a room with him; Dave worked as a lighting guy in the rock and roll business. He was often away on tour. I was now in motorcycle dispatch, riding during the week, and at weekends I was away as a reservist with the Parachute Regiment, having got through their selection process. After an airborne exercise on Sunday, I would often come back to the flat still in my uniform and camo face paint to find my flatmates skinning up big joints in the flat. Paul was hilarious on Monday, getting into his suit after a stoned weekend to head to the city. He's now high up in the city.

Dave was working mainly for a company called TTR, run by Richard, an American. Together they supplied all the equipment for touring bands. Steve told me they were looking for somebody to work in the equipment yard, so I went for an interview. The yard was based in West Ham, next to a chemical plant in Edwin Shirley trucking yard. Coincidently they did all the rock and roll trucking. One small problem - the trucks didn't always fit under the low railway bridge, so the drivers deflated tyres to get them under the bridge. John, the boss, interviewed me. John led a group of unusual characters who worked there getting stuff ready for tours. Occasionally a road crew would come in and set things up.

I repaired road boxes and painted aluminium trusses. The boss got the cables, lights and rigging packed up and checked in. The kit was fundamental in the early 80s. In essence, an aluminium bolt-together framework with lights attached in rows of six. The gel frames were of different colours in front. All this was controlled by a simple fade in/out lighting desk. All the lights had to be hand-focused once they were in the air.

There seemed to be a Rota system on who would go on tour, and Mick was next in line.

However, I arrived one morning, and John called me in. "There's a tour starting in a few weeks, and Mick doesn't want to go. Do you fancy it?" I had done eight months in the yard, it was relaxed, with good company, and I was keen. It was a world tour with Genesis for a year, starting in Dallas with rehearsals; I had a short time to pack up in London and go.

I arrived in Dallas with a rucksack, a sizeable black stage drape stuffed into it, and a few clothes fitted into the remaining space. Richard met me, and his first words were, "Have you got the drape?" We drove to his place. All he had in the house was a fridge and a few chairs; I ended up sleeping on the floor wrapped in an old blanket while he worked most of the night on his computer.

Luckily, rehearsals started a few days later, and I got a hotel room. We had five in our crew - two Americans, Dave and Cosmo, three Brits, Ian, myself and our crew chief, Charlie. My first job was to paint the aluminium truss with black epoxy - I managed to convince the other American crew that I was so good that they flew me worldwide to hand paint trusses!

Genesis had invested in a new lighting system called Vari-lite, a light that could pan, tilt, rotate, and have a range of colour changes. The truss could also move into different configurations with a computer-controlled motor system; it was revolutionary and was a game-changer. Our job was to build this system. It was a big rig - lots of moving triangles of truss running inside a sizeable octagonal truss. We rehearsed in Dallas for four weeks, and then we were off. The first stop was Detroit on a 4-month

American tour. We worked long hours at the start, but as the tour progressed, we got more efficient. We had big tour buses for travel; it was exciting and fun most of the time.

We toured big venues in North and South America, Canada, Australia and New Zealand. We played to over 3 million people. We were now on our way to Europe - our tour manager and ex-rodeo star and charismatic boss, Mo, wanted to do New York to Paris, back to back, one show in America, the next show in France the following evening .this was the first time with a show this size. We finished at Giant's Stadium, and as the gear came down, the crew loaded it onto trucks to get put on cargo planes at JFK airport. They then chartered Concorde for the team and the band to catch the freight up and be there in Paris to start setting up the show. The flight on Concorde was one big party. Champagne flowed, and so did the drugs done in the toilets; the aircrew just pretty much left us to it, although I remember our crew still trying to use the toilets as the plane landed. We finished the tour at Wembley Stadium.

After the tour, I went off climbing for a couple of months, followed by more touring, working as a rigger. I travelled with the Pet Shop Boys, Springsteen and Depeche Mode. People worked hard and partied hard - it was still wild, with many interesting characters. One band tried to give me my tour bonus in cocaine!

I did a Rolling Stones tour in the '90s and was working rigging the roofs on the stages. It was a massive logistical job, with up to 70 Artic trucks of equipment per show leapfrogging each other all over Europe. The stages were 300ft wide and 90ft tall. Health and Safety didn't really exist, and we worked on scaffold boards and hauled steel up and down. I rigged the roof on chain motors and giant steel cable. The Production Team for this was immense. A wide walkway of aluminium at 90ft, massive inflatable Women and dogs, and a stage that was supposed to represent an Urban Jungle.

The walkway was big and wide so that Mick Jagger could go up and dance on the walkway.

He didn't like heights much, and the best we could get him to do was leave the elevator and dance at the side of the tower. I went up with him and sometimes had to lie down, holding onto his ankles to make him feel safer while his top half swayed away to 'Sympathy for the Devil'.

The tour was great, and although the band were getting on in age, we partied. I built a bar under the stage, and production gave us a few hundred dollars for alcohol at the end of the shows. The security guys gave backstage passes to all the most attractive girls they saw. The band rarely turned up, so they must have been disappointed to find the road crew only. I built a bar and worked behind, it was more fun, and I got to know people better. The bar travelled with us, and I remember seeing a road box with some beautiful wood in it, and this looked perfect for the top of the bar, so I sawed it up and hammered it to the old pallets I had been using. That night Gerry, the production manager, was there, and I poured him his usual Jack and Coke. He was admiring the bar top and asked me where I got the wood. I told him about the old road box that I found it in; finishing his drink, he told me it was Jagger's spare dance floor, and if they ever needed it, he would fire me. In the meantime, he told me the bar was a great idea and asked for a double!

I continued touring, mainly in Europe, staying in tour buses and hotels and going on

**ON CONCORDE FOR THE FINAL LEG OF
THE GENESIS TOUR**

climbing trips in between. I travelled with all manner of acts - Ah-Ha, Simply Red, Chris de Burgh. Some were easy but tedious. The Chris de Burgh tour had a great crew with multiple dates and time off; we skied, paddled and had our bikes on the trucks, so we were active. The show was boring, but we amused ourselves by operating big spotlights during the show. Putting pin spots on the bands bollocks, when Chris introduced them., from the spotlights we were running We went a bit too far one night - when Chris did a boring monologue to add a song, we got the sound boys to put the sound of one of the crew snoring on the bus through the central sound system. Chris stormed off, and we all got a proper bollocking.

I did staging for Simply red, building and suspending the outdoor roof. Thirty tons of Aluminum structure suspended on steel cables and chain motor hoists. The rest of the stage on either side involved red drapes going up and down during the show. I was asked at the last minute before showtime to rig something and didn't realise till I was watching the show that I had put a scaffolding pole in the way of some of the drapes and ruined one of the show's highlights. I managed to disappear before they worked it out.

It was still fun, but the accountants seemed to be taking over. Some of the new crew were not the same; they were more content to watch computer games than have a bit of a laugh. It was all getting

THE JOURNEY NOT THE DESTINATION

more serious. The last tour was Paul McCartney in South America. I got a call to replace somebody. I had to rig giant screens on either side of the stage; these moved up and down on motors, and it was a challenging and complicated job. I was doing long days before I got it sorted, up and down the giant towers. I didn't get much support from an old crew boss friend, and it all seemed a bit too corporate. I was saving money to go on a trip to Torres Del Paine in Patagonia afterwards, and the crew knew I had cash.

I was heading off to Patagonia with a couple of lads I worked with building the stages. We were leaving all the Rock and Roll madness behind with a bit of cash and some camping gear and no real plan other than to have a good time.

I gave up the rigging full time so that I could work in the outdoors. I did the occasional exciting job for the challenge and the money. I started working with stunt riggers on films through some contacts. I worked on some of the Batman movies. The first job was in Cardington in one of the old airship hangers. They had built Gotham city in it, and I remember walking around this massive set between takes. The stunt riggers were very impressive, improvising kit for the stunts and very professional.

When I got called to go to Aberdeen to work on another Batman movie at short notice, I jumped at the chance. I arrived and met Dave, the crew chief. Dave was a real gentleman and a pleasure to work alongside. However, before I knew it, I was straight onto the back of a Hercules aircraft, and we were taking off. Dave said he would explain the

job as we went, and looking at all the setup, I would have to learn fast.

We got up to Nine thousand feet, and we were lowering two stunt guys out of the back ramp of the plane on a single 70 feet rope and going to winch them back up. It was the film's opening sequence where the bad guys were being lowered out of one plane to a smaller one beneath to rescue another bad-guy boss, and this was a practice run. We got them out, ok. I had then to move the ropes onto an electric winch and rewind them up. Unfortunately, Hercules planes mainly work on hydraulics, and we couldn't get the power to run the winch, and it kept cutting out. So we flew the aircraft towards an airfield with these poor stunt guys dragged behind, and Dave told me to go to the end of the ramp and wave a high visibility vest at the two pissed off looking stunt boys as a signal to cut away from the ropes and operate their parachutes. I had only been on the job for an hour; what was going to happen next!?

The next day one of the stunt guys broke his leg on landing his parachute, and on day three, one of them crashed into a residential house roof and got his leg stuck and had to be rescued by the homeowner. The press had a field day calling him a prat man.

I only had two weeks on the job as I was going off on an expedition. Every day was a challenge, and I was never sure about what was going to happen. These guys worked at the top end of challenging environments. I thought that after all this, expedition challenges would seem like a rest.

CHAPTER
**THREE**

# FLYING WITHOUT WINGS

THE JOURNEY NOT THE DESTINATION

BATTALION JUMP WITH FULL KIT I AM
CARRYING A SMG TUCKED UNDER MY
RESERVE AS I HAVE THE RADIO SET

# "I had always had a fascination with flying,

not in a plane but falling out of one; with the added requirement, I could repeat the experience. So the only viable option was parachuting or skydiving.

I was living in London with little money and motorcycle dispatch riding to pay bills. I often went all over the capital. One day outside Duke of Yorks Barracks in King's rd, I saw a poster about the 10th battalion Parachute regiment.

It was an Army reserve unit, and it paid you as well. So the following week, I turned up at one company barracks at White City. I was a little naïve; I knew a little about the regiment's reputation, but not any basic idea of what lay ahead before you got anywhere near an aircraft.

What lay ahead was six months of being shouted at and run ragged, culminating in P company. A race carrying a heavy stretcher as a team; 10-mile battle marches in complete kit taking a heavy pack and rifle, A log race, a high-level scaffolding assault course with no nets and finally, milling. In a boxing contest where you had to give out and receive punishment, somebody broke my nose in the first minute. Still, as long as you stay on your feet to the end, you passed.

After doing all this, you got the coveted Red beret, but you still weren't accepted until you got your parachute wings.

The next stop was Brize Norton and The RAF parachute training school. The RAF approach to training was a little different, no shouting, just a bemused look that they were dealing with a bunch of morons. We had to do loads of drills, on bits of specialized kit, including the Knacker Cracker, no guesses what that damaged and finally seven jumps, 6 out of a Hercules C130 Plane and one ballon jump.

The aircraft jumps were full of noise, shouting and being pushed and shoved out into a 125mph slipstream and then silence, you have little time to think, and you follow drills. The balloon is entirely different. A wicker basket on a cable with the RAF despatcher chatting away, lifting a small metal gate and inviting you to step out. It was terrifying the Despatchers have a prize for anybody who can get a hard-on during the balloon ascent; God knows how you prove it.

I did an American parachute course one year, where we jumped each others kit. The Elite American Rangers we were working with refused to do the balloon and send their black cooks up first to check it out as it was only 600 feet up. You just dropped straight down, leaving your stomach in your mouth.

There is a story about the Gurkhas asked if they were happy being airborne troops dropping out of the aircraft at 600feet. The senior sergeants went off to talk to the men and came back and said they were ok with it but wanted to jump at 100ft. The officers told them it was too low for the parachutes, at which the Gurkhas said, oh, we have parachutes!

We used to jump in Sticks of 20 -30 men on each side of the Hercules, often with a container with all our gear, guns, ammo and food, strapped to our legs and then lower this on a rope once the parachute had opened, landing with it still attached would shatter your legs. Our Regimental Sergeant major didn't really like jumping but had to do one a year to claim his parachute bounty.

Before the jump, he would talk about how he didn't want anybody near him in the sky. I happened to be opposite him on the other stick on this jump. The RAF despatchers try and stagger the two rows of men out of the plane. I went out the door, and my parachute opened, and I could see the RSM beneath me looking happy; unfortunately, I drifted right over the top of him, and his canopy took all my air, my parachute collapsed, and I ended up face to face with him. He screamed in surprise and told me to fuck off, and I drifted away, saluting.

Luckily I was camouflaged with face paint, so when he all lined us up after the jump to find out who it was, he couldn't identify me.

We did water jumps, night jumps, and jumped at Arnhem to commemorate the regiment's famous Bridge Too Far battle. People often hurt themselves as the parachutes only had essential steerage ability, and landings were pretty hard.

I took up Sports Skydiving. When I left the regiment, I had to retrain and borrow a bit of money to buy a second-hand Square parachute. Sports skydiving was a whole new ball game, steerable and softer landings, and I spent the next few years jumping at weekends.

We had a Pilot at one of the jump centres who hated dogs, and we managed to get him in a parachute harness simulator suspended in a hanger then let a friendly Doberman. He played around with him for half an hour, his yells, swearing and screaming echoed as we shut the door.

He calmed down, but the following weekend we were all jumping out of Skyvan, holding about 20 skydivers and the back ramp opening, and you all pile out. As we were coming in for the final run at 13.000 feet, he gets out of the pilot seat, walks past, shouts you bastards and jumps out of the back with a parachute. We all sit there in silence, not knowing what to do when another skydiver takes off his parachute and takes control. He tells us not to fuck with the pilot again, and we all get on with the jump.

I managed to do some jumps out of a DC3 or Dakota in the U.S. at Z-Hills parachute centre in Florida, The DC3 was the plane used in the second world war in all the significant airborne drops, and only a few were still in use. The safety brief was a little different; if you landed near the edge of the airfield near the swamps, you were to keep an eye out for the alligators and run in a Zig-Zag direction because the alligators have difficulty in changing direction quickly.

I stopped jumping and left my parachute at the Parachute Centre. I spent more time climbing and paddling; it was challenging to fit it all in. However, while working in the mountains, I saw many Paragliders flying about, which looked amazing.

I booked a few lessons with a local operator called Mark and loved it and bought a Paraglider, This was in the 90s, and the sport was still relatively new. The mountains of Snowdonia were quite challenging flying, and I often went into work early to fly off our local mountain Moel Siabhod,

I decided to get a few more skills and decided to go on an SUV course, all about getting your paraglider into difficulties and sorting out problems. It was in Turkey at a beach resort called Oladeniz, full of tourists soaking up the sun. Mark had driven a battered old land rover across from the U.K. with another instructor Jocky, and they were running the course.

It was a mixed bunch of people, mainly from the Peak district with small rolling hills rather than mountains. The first day we drove to the top of Babadag mountain around 7000ft from the sea. It was a rough track to the top in the Landrover, with the bonnet removed to stop it from overheating. On top of the mountain top was a rugged slope leading to a massive drop. Nobody wanted to go first. Mark asked me to step up as I had done some mountain flying. I laid the paraglider out on the floor, acutely aware of the short, uneven ground I had to run down to get the thing in the air before the significant drop.

The take-off was one of the worst Mark had seen, he told me later and hadn't inspired confidence in the rest of the team, and two took the land rover back down.

I was now in the air enjoying the fantastic scenery looking down over the sea. My peaceful enjoyment was short-lived as Jocky sunbathed with his girlfriend on the rescue boat with a radio. He told me to do some big spiral dives and collapse my canopy. I pulled on the lines, grabbed handfuls, and started plummeting to the sea, waiting for his command to release it.

It was a terrifying first day, the air rushing past and the g forces in the spiral dives. I found myself giggling with nervous laughter back to the beach. The flying was pretty intense; you soared above the mountain's ridges picking up thermals and then flying over the emerald sea and performing terrifying manoeuvres. A few of the flyers were learning at a high comfort level, often disappearing over the back of the mountain and returning a day later, having landed in a village and had to catch the local buses or taxis back. The instructors seemed pretty laid back about it, as it was a regular occurrence.

Some flyers regularly crashed into the beach, knocking the Harley Davidson motorbike off its place above the Harley bar. Some smashed through the wicker roofing of the restaurants to the surprise of the diners. It seemed ok and part of the vibe of the place.

I came back from the trip with new confidence and crashed on my first flight back home. I stalled the paraglider trying out something, dropped straight to the ground, narrowly missing some boulders, and knocked myself out. After a few minutes, I came around, and my girlfriend took me to the local hospital in Bangor. They put me in a cubicle, and after a few minutes, a young female in a white coat told me to undress and gave me the cough test with cold hands. I hasten to add. She smiled and said to me that I looked ok left. A few

**PARAGLIDING OVER OLA DENIZ IN TURKEY. THE LANDING SITE IS THE BEACH, IF NOT THE WATER!**

minutes later, a male doctor came in and asked why I was undressed, and I tried to explain; he looked confused and examined my head area, told me to get dressed and discharged me, saying if I had any dizzy or unusual symptoms to come straight back in.

I told my girlfriend about the encounters, and she said it was imaginary due to the knock on the head. The following weekend we were in a local bar in Bangor. I noticed a group of girls all dressed up for a night out, drinking and smoking at the bar. There was the female doctor slightly worse for wear. I ordered a drink and asked the Barman if they had a doctor's night out. He laughed and said no as they were the hospital cleaners.

# AN AFRICAN ADVENTURE

# "It's 1987, and I am at Heathrow airport to meet up with Nick,

our guide and three other clients ready to head off to Kenya to try and climb Mount Kenya. I have never met the others before, George, Margaret and Richard.

First impressions are always exciting and often shape your opinions of people, sometimes wrongly. My reaction to George was that he was a chatterbox, and I thought he would drive me to distraction, and he is now one of my closest friends.

I was still touring with bands and had limited time but consistent cash flow, so I had signed up for this trip as I had never climbed at this altitude. Mount Kenya is over 5000m, and we hoped to attempt one of the famous ice climbs. Nick was a British mountain guide, and he had organised this and would be guiding us on the climb. I was still relatively inexperienced, and Nick had taught me before. After the climb, I hoped to catch up with my brother working as a safari guide in the country.

There are a few trails into the mountain, and we chose to walk in via Naro more trail and left Nairobi with our local guide Sammy and porters and the following day started the trek. We were walking through lush forests, and the scenery was stunning. That evening, we camped near a lodge, and we played football with the locals; unfortunately, Nick had his camera pinched; this was the start of a bad trip.

We had to be careful to be slow in our ascent

to avoid altitude sickness, and we took our time getting to the top hut near the mountain, called the Austrian hut. That evening, a porter and I made an ascent of the trekking peak, Point Lenana, as I felt pretty good with the altitude. The others were going to ascend it the following day; it was a straightforward walk to a flat summit.

That night Nick felt unwell and had all the symptoms of altitude sickness, so we decided to get him down as soon as possible. Pulmonary or cerebral oedema is a severe condition and can be fatal if not acted on immediately. Sammy and some of the guides left to take him down the Chogoria trail to a lower hut. Generally, if you descend straight away, recovery follows; we hoped this would be the case.

We now had lost our climbing guide; we ascended Point Lenana again with the rest of the group, then descended to the other side of the mountain where the ice climbs were. We hoped Nick might recover and come and join us in a few days. However, it became clear that this wasn't going to happen, and we had to make some decisions.

I was keen to give the Ice window Route a go. George wanted to stay with Margaret, but Richard seemed eager. So on new years eve, we bivied under some rocks near the climb base and got up at 3 am to start climbing.

We moved up a diagonal snow ramp that

led up to the glacier overhang cave's ice window. I then had to smash through some icicles and swing out onto the vertical diamond couloir ice climb. I swung around on my ice axes and climbed some steep ice to get onto the top glacier, then Richard followed as I belayed him. The sun was now on the Diamond glacier, and we could feel the altitude, but we carried on up to the col between the two summits of Nelion and Bation, aptly called the Gates of Mist, as the cloud rolled in. We reached the summit late afternoon, pretty tired and dehydrated, and luckily there is a small aluminium shelter on the mountain.

It had lots of stickers on from expedition teams from military to foreign climbers, but in the middle of the door was a label for Anglesey scaffolding, local to where I lived in Wales, how the mighty fall.

We got a brew on and decided to get some sleep and descend in the morning. Richard was suffering the following day, so I set up all the abseils to get off the mountain from the Austrian hut side. It all went pretty smoothly, and Richard looked better when we got down to the hut, and we carried on descending to where the others were still camping. George said he had seen us crossing the Diamond glacier and then lost us in the clouds.

We felt very pleased; it had been a gamble, an adventure and my first time on a big mountain. It would provide me with confidence for the future, climbing with somebody I barely knew and, after this trip, would never see again.

We left the following day to head down the chogaria trail to check on Nick. We met him halfway down on his way up. He looked terrible, with a swollen face and his clothes ripped.

He had recovered from the altitude sickness but now had a tooth abscess, and some Italians had left the door of the hut open he was in, and the baboons got in and ripped up his clothes. The magic and mystic of Africa had worn off for him, and he was heading home, and Richard was going with him.

I had plenty of time left, and George and Margaret were up for some exploring. We hired Sammy as our guide and went travelling and climbing. One memorable day George and I headed into Hells Gate, a giant climbing cliff. I have memories of the heat, loose rock and baboons climbing around us. To top it off, we summited at dusk then had to walk back to camp with the sound of all those big animals you don't want to meet all around us.

We headed back to Nairobi, and brother Howard and his friend Malcolm met us for a drink. They arrived in a battered old landrover and had already had a few beers. Both looked the part of a safari guide, my brother being the skinnier version of Daktari. Malcolm was a big south African, loud with that lazy kind of racism and was horrified when he found out we were staying in the locals part of town.

Luckily he wasn't on the next part of the Trip, George and Margaret had flown home, and Howard picked me up the next day to head to Amboseli game reserve with the rest of his crew.

We were picking up the clients who had flown from the U.K and then dropped them of in a jungle camp in the park. Unfortunately, our vehicle broke down just out of Nairobi. By the time we had fixed it and got to the park, it was now dark, and we had to bribe the guards at the gate to let us in.

The clients had been left in the camp alone, expecting us to be there shortly after being dropped off. By the time we got there, they were all huddled around a campfire with noises of wild animals circling and were so glad to see us rather than angry.

We put the tents up, and in the morning, our cooks and porters looked after the clients as we packed up camp and headed off. The Park wildlife was excellent, and the clients assumed I was staff, although I had paid a reduced rate, and I enjoyed helping the team.

One camp we had was notorious for an inquisitive elephant, and sure enough, he came rummaging through the field late one night. My brother was in one of the female client's tents, providing that little extra professional service and came running out trying to get dressed. Our cook threw a mallet at the elephant, which promptly picked it up and threw it back at him, knocking him out. Eventually, we got in the land rover and drove it out of camp.

The cook had a massive lump on his head the following day. He was bald, and we stuck a criss-cross plaster on it and nicknamed him Mr Mallet.

The vehicle frequently broke down, and the clients had to push, but they all took it as part of the adventure. The final part of the trip was to take them to a luxury 5-star hotel in Nairobi. But as we drove, the concentrated orange juice started leaking from the roof rack. With the truck windows open, this quietly coated most of the clients, and then all the dust stuck to them. We were in the front and safe, and they seemed unaware of what was happening.

We drove to the reception area, and we hopped out to check them in. Although we were grubby, the concierge in this immaculate foyer welcomed us.

However, when our clients started walking in, he changed his tune. They looked like vagrants, all resemblance to western holidaymakers erased. He rushed from behind the desk and tried to get them to their rooms as quickly as possible to keep them away from the other guests.

I think the final insult was as we left, all the cabbages fell off our roof rack into the immaculate gardens as we waved out the window.

I had been in Kenya for six weeks, and I had two very different experiences. Both had made it an unforgettable holiday.

AVOIDING THE DEBRIS COMING
OFF THE TOP OF THE WALL AS THE
SUN HEATED UP

# THE BROOM OF GOD

**PINGO VALLEY, TORRES DEL PAINE NATIONAL PARK**

# "Patagonia is at the Tip of South America.

Torres del Paines Jagged peaks and big steep walls rise out of the flat plains, like a massive open hand exploding out of the ground. I had been invited on an expedition here at the last moment by Mike Turner, who I knew well as we had come through our climbing qualifications together. The other team members were Louise, who I knew well, and Martin Doyle, who I didn't

Mike and Louise were already a well-established partnership in the expedition world. Martin was the Chief Instructor at Plas y Brenin and had already had a few big walls under his belt. I was the novice. I remember reading John Middledorfs big wall book on the plane to Santiago, hoping not to make a fool of myself on the trip.

I arrived a few days ahead of the others; I staggered out of Santiago airport with a haul bag with 500m of rope and gear. These were the days when you could get away with it on airlines. I took another flight to Punta Arenas and then a bus to Puerto Natales, and I settled in. I had to go to the park, pay a climbing permit of $600 and sort out horses to ferry our gear. Pablo was the local horseman to transport our equipment. He and his partner who lived in a shack in the park were suspicious of me until I mentioned I knew Paul Pritchard. Another climber who had used Pablo's services, and then all was cool.

**Cuernos Norte**

Fistful of Dollars
A2, E5, 6a
800m
24 Pitches

Olly Sanders          Martin Doyle
Mike Twid Turner    Louise Thomas

**STEEP CRACK AIDING WITH ALL
THE GEAR NEEDED**

The others arrived. We headed into Pingo valley, walking with the horses on a rough trail. Nobody had climbed in here; hence, the track was indistinct. Eventually, we found an area suitable for a camp. Our main objective was the unclimbed south tower. We spent the next few days exploring options until we decided to try a new route on Cuenos Norte due to the lack of features at the south tower's start.

We had a snowy approach to the wall's initial slabs, and Twid and Louise started the climbing. We would take over after a couple of days. They free-climbed the slabs and started fixing the ropes. By the time we came to take over, they had established themselves 100m up the steep wall above. Our problem was ascending fixed ropes quickly to avoid the ice and debris falling from the summit onto

the slabs. Once we were on the wall itself, it was overhanging enough for it to miss us.

Being a relative novice at aid climbing, I thought Martin would start, and I would pick it up as I went. No chance Martin told me to get on with it. A day of ripped hands, poor technique and exhaustion at the end with slow progress up the wall. I had, however, learnt from all my mistakes with a bit of input shouted from below.

It was a slow and laborious job; you would place a piece of gear, test it, then clip-in two nylon ladders and work your way up the ladders till you attach into the kit with your harness. You could then reach as high as possible in this unstable position to place the next piece and repeat the process.

The crack systems ran out above us, so we had to do a king swing. We placed some protection at the

**THE OVERHANGING NATURE OF THE CLIMBING**

end of the last crack, and I lowered Martin down. He then began running back and forth until he was able to swing and reach another crack system. It was terrifying to watch him swing 500m above the ground and realise I was up next!

We had to place bolts with a hand-held driver, which you hammered and twisted to drill into the granite. Once again, with little knowledge of this procedure. I almost buggered up the drill. Twid and Louise came back after a few days, they were disappointed with our progress and furious about the drill episode, but I was learning on the job.

We carried on with this routine swopping over at the sharp end until we eventually reached a small narrow ledge about halfway. Here we all joined Twid and Louise in a porta ledge and martin, and I squeezed onto the ledge tied in as we slept so we

didn't roll off. It was a 500m drop. I always slept well on the wall with the spare ropes as a pillow, mainly because I was knackered.

I made a mistake early on of not doing up my jacket when I was aid climbing. All the grit worked its way down into my underpants and trapped by my harness, so I got a bad case of nappy rash, which I could only sort out back on the ledge.

We were on the wall for two weeks; we hauled up the gear in tough bags and had to carry water, food, stoves etc., It was hard graft, bodyweight hauling all the equipment and ascending fixed lines. The fixed ropes took a hammering on the tough granite, and I was frequently putting duck tape around worn ropes. Not to repair them, but to take away visual clues of ropes that were getting weaker

Leaving the ledge on the final push was always

**SLEEPING ON THE LEDGE TIED INTO
THE HAND LINE**

exciting, with a diagonal rope to ascend and a giant swing out into nothing. Twid managed to free climb the last pitches, and as we had run out of static rope, we ended up ascending the ropes on 9mm dynamic rope. Once you put your weight on them and they had stretched, they looked like shoelaces. We had already had loads of wear on the other fixed lines.

We topped out of the vertical world and onto a completely different type of rock, a pile of loose and broken ground. We decided it wasn't worth the risk of ascending this to the actual summit a short distance away on less steep climbing and started to set up anchors for the Descent. We had an 800M to descend, with all the fixed rope to clear as we went. It was going to be a long and complicated job. I made the mistake of chucking a load of the rope off the wall. Only to be told that was for lowering bags. so I ended up strapped to the bags clearing them during the lowering, I vowed never to tidy up again!

It was amazing how bad some of the ropes

THE JOURNEY NOT THE DESTINATION

LOOKING DOWN ON HALWAY LEDGE READY
FOR MORNING ASCENT

THE HALFWAY LEDGE ON THE CLIMB

**BIG WALL HANDS AFTER 3 WEEKS**

had suffered damage, and when we finally got to the snow slopes, it was a massive bunch of rope spaghetti. We were so tired we just dragged the huge bunch down the snow slope back to camp. When we got back to camp, Louise got the whiskey bottle hidden from Martin and me. Which we had vainly spent hours searching for when she and Twid were climbing, and we chuckled about how close we had been to discover the whisky.

We called the route a Fistful of Dollars due to the Peak fee we had to pay. Graded at A2 E5 6a 800m 24 pitches, the first route in Pingo Valley. We were lucky to experience the park before it started to change. The old Refugio's were being knocked down and replaced with modern type Bunkhouses. Pablo was evicted to make way for more tourist accommodation.

The team headed back to the UK, and I stayed for a couple of days to wind up the Expedition paperwork in Puerto Natales. I arrived back in Heathrow and then drove straight to Plas y Brenin to interview for a 10-year job. Luckily Martin was on the panel, and you could say I had slept with the boss on ledges on the wall for the last month, so I got the job!

# CHAPTER
## SIX

# HOUSE OF
# KINGS

## "It is 1992, and I am getting tired of the travel and Rigging,

and I have just finished a Paul McCartney tour and a tough job. There is a Senior full-time instructor job advertised at Plas y Brenin, The National Mountain Centre.

I was also missing one qualification to meet the job criteria, an advanced white water kayak award. I managed to pass this a day before I left for Patagonia and posted the application at the airport.

Twid and I had worked through the Instructional awards together, and we did our mountain instructor together. We scraped through one of the mountain days; Twid reckoned he missed one of the night navigation test markers because a horse had come out the dark and run of with it. With that much front, he was well on his way to becoming a mountain guide.

Our winter mountain leader test was also unforgettable. We spent a week before climbing rather than navigating, ticking off classic grade 5 routes such as Ravens Gully, Poachers falls and Central Buttress on Beinn Eighe.

The team gathered on the first night were familiar faces, Louise, two friends, George Manley and Tim Bird and a policeman from London called Fraser. For the 3-day expedition, we went to Creag Megaidh and walked into the dark to build snow holes in a feature called the window, a flat area between two mountains. The following day, we made some more snow holes beneath the famous climbing cliffs and went navigating. Our assessors were Malcolm Creasy and Marcus Bailee. As we were walking back into the Coire, we spotted some Avalanche activity. A large gully splits the Cliffs, and we spotted the debris and a figure. As we walked around, we came across another casualty who we knew, Tim Snaith. He had been climbing with Paul farmer and had forgotten his harness but had still decided to climb Smiths Gully, a challenging ice climb of the cliffs with the rope tied around his waist. He had fallen off the second pitch and luckily landed at the bottom and had not pulled Paul of the inadequate belay. He had injured his leg and had a black eye, courtesy of some Irish climbers who were also on the climb. Tim had flown over the top of one of them, almost pulling him off, and when the Irish lad got down, He punched Tim for being stupid, then set off for help.

Mobile phones didn't exist then, and it was at least an hour and a half to the nearest farm. We carried on around the cliff's base to find Marcus, one of the assessors was dealing with a casualty. The guy had a compound fracture of his femur but was sitting up in the avalanche debris. He kept asking about his partner, so Frazer and I were dispatched to go up and look.

We climbed up the massive snow debris and soon saw a pair of boots sticking out of the snow. We dug down but soon realised that there was little hope.

The next few hours seemed to fly by, and we tried to keep the news from the other climber. Soon we could hear the Helicopter flying up the valley, and they picked up Tim first. The casualty and finally the fatality, Frazer as a policeman provided dark humour to the situation, somebody who had dealt with this many times.

The climbers had been in the wrong place at the wrong time, making a decision that would change the course of their lives; it was a sobering reminder. The assessment we were on would qualify us to lead people in winter, where we would have to make decisions for the less experienced and keep them safe.

We went back to the snow holes to eat as darkness fell; the events shook everybody. The assessors were in the next spot, and we could hear a heated discussion, but soon they came and told us to get ready as we continued with the assessment. Nobody was happy with this, but we had spent years preparing for this, so we got on with it. In retrospect, I think this was the right decision; we may have had to deal with this for real and carry on and get our group safely off the mountains. This episode was 30 years ago, and I wonder if the assessors would make the same decision in today's climate of health and safety.

We navigated through the night, with the first rays of light bathing us in its golden glow. It seemed the best sunrise I had ever seen as we came down to the minibus after the events of the day before.

I have been working in the winter ever since, going to Scotland for the annual pilgrimage. I got the job at Pyb and started working. It was like sink or swim in those days, and the culture was if you are senior Staff, then get on with it; there wasn't a support culture as there is today. It suited me, but you learnt on the job, mainly making the right decisions and some poor ones, that fortunately, didn't have massive consequences.

It's demanding work, physically and mentally, as anybody who works Scottish winters will tell you, but I loved it. Fresh tracks, Summit views, battling conditions. The Staff climbed together, and there was a real buzz with the people you worked with and the clients. This time was before the internet, so we partied and drank with the clients and our peers and played hard and worked hard.

However, other instructors and climbers have accidents and deaths, which remind you not to get complacent. I didn't dwell on it too much. I accepted it as part of the job and tried to be supportive of new Staff and change the culture a little.

The work was always exciting and varied, working on recreational courses or training and assessing people for instructional awards. We ran

Sea Kayaking expeditions to Scotland and often met the clients in a car park in Scotland with only a rough idea of their ability level and headed off for a six-day journey. We sometimes had to deal with weak paddlers in challenging conditions. I had three Geordie lads who had been economical with the truth and one who couldn't swim. He told me, however, he would float, not flap.

On another trip, I forgot a Sea kayak and had to leave the other staff member and a client at a service station while I dashed back to the Centre. We arrived late in Glencoe and went into The Claichaig Inn and joined a cailee. We woke up laid out in The minibus and had to rush to meet the rest of the clients on Skye. I managed to appear very organised with a clipboard. When it came to the Introductions, I dreaded what the client who had driven up with us would say. However, he introduced himself and told the rest they were in the hands of two consummate professionals.

We were Plas y Brenin all rolled into a Minibus and trailer. Sometimes we didn't ring in for days as mobiles weren't around much. We relied on shipping forecasts on the radio to make decisions, and we had a vhf radio for emergencies.

I learnt more about decision making and looking after people from these experiences than anything else I had done. It always felt like a proper adventure. The clients and Staff all bonded together to make it work. It was challenging, but it was brilliant times with great people.

The Centre had gone through an upheaval when I started, almost taken over by a leisure centre company. Luckily, we had friends in high places and were saved by a consortium of National outdoor councils, who created a Mountain Training Trust

to run us.

We had a new boss Iain, a mountain guide and straight talker. I liked him from the start. He left you to get on with your job and got on with his, concentrating on getting new business and running the Centre.

Looking back, we had excellent staff training trips abroad, a great social scene and Staff members doing impressive ground-breaking expeditions worldwide. You would often bump into a staff member in the locker room who had been away and have a chat. Only to find out from somebody else, they had done the first ascent on a remote mountain area.

Staff worked hard and played hard, but it didn't feel like a job, just doing all the things you loved doing. However, you were instructors at the peak of the profession working at a world-renowned centre, in challenging conditions keeping people safe.

Like any Institution, we got stick, elitist Staff, too well funded, not in touch. Honestly, I ignored it; some may have been true, but generally, the Staff were passionate and committed. All the Staff are like a big family and care about the place. Over recent years, we have had a management that hasn't fully appreciated this, coming from a business background. The strength of the place is in the Staff, not the building.

Will it survive? I have always been optimistic that it will, hopefully, keeping Outdoor Education's ethos. With so many local authority centres shutting and depriving young people of that outdoor experience in their formative years, national centres must survive to train the next generation of outdoor professionals to keep carrying the torch.

WINTER MOUNTAIN LEADER
ASSESMENT IN GREAG MEAGAIDH
RETURNING TO SNOW HOLES

ARRIVING AT KULUSUK WITH ALL OUR
GEAR FOR THE MONTH

# CHAPTER
## SEVEN

# OUR FIRST BIG ARCTIC EXPEDITION

# "Leo and I worked together regularly.

We had built a reputation as a sea kayak double act. We were running all Plas y Brenin sea kayak expeditions. We were keen and ran trips to Scotland, Ireland, Outer Hebrides and elsewhere. We would often turn up and meet clients in these places and hope the booking team had asked if they could paddle. Sometimes they were economical with the truth—one time, we had three geordie lads who had never kayaked before but had blagged it. One of them couldn't swim. "I float, and I don't flap", he told me.

Some didn't realise how committing a six-day kayak trip can be in Scotland—sometimes caught out by storms, we had to get up and paddle early to miss lousy weather. Tents flattened, and people capsized, but somehow it all worked. We had plenty of laughs with the most exceptional people. Groups made up of folk from all walks of life thrown together for a week's adventure. Leo and I properly learned our trade and how to make the right decisions. We had little contact with the centre until the end of the trips, as mobile signals were weak in the 90s.

Whilst on these trips, we dreamt of other destinations and adventures. As we shared a tent, we had plenty of time to chat. I had been on some climbing expeditions that had received funding, and I reckoned we could get some funds from the Welsh Sports council expedition fund. Leo suggested Greenland as a warm-up for an idea we had to paddle to the Magnetic North pole in the future.

We managed to get some funding from sport wales. Then through a contact at a private school, we located some kayaks in the Ammasilak area. The kayaks were there to encourage the local population to use kayaks again. The deal was we would get the boats for free if we did some coaching with the local children.

We were going to Ammasalak on the east coast of Greenland. The plan was to head north to find Gino Watkins's grave, a famous explorer and kayaker. He had died in the 1930s at the age of 25 exploring in his kayak, and his body was never found. Money was tight, and I remember Leo ringing his mum at the airport to try and borrow a bit of cash. We took as much kit as we could. I think I had 30 snickers bars in my hand luggage. We eventually arrived at Kulusuk, a short helicopter ride from the airport. As we walked up the hill to the campsite, we almost got wiped out by a pick-up truck dragging a dead seal up the road to feed dogs. The truck missed us, but it was close with the seal.

We spent the next few days trying to locate the kayaks. After various false leads, we eventually found them stored under a house. They were sea kayaks based on a traditional Inuit sea kayak with a small round cockpit to get in and out. They had round hatches to store food under rubber covers. We had bought 23 days of boil in the bag food with us in our hold luggage, and we supplemented this at local stores. I had asked Leo what he wanted to eat from the meals. There were seven options in the range; one was chicken tikka masala. He decided that this was his only choice for three weeks. To make it worse, every time we were about to eat, Leo reminded me it was his favourite again tonight.

On the third day, he managed to spill it all over the tent; to this day, the smell of chicken tikka makes me wince.

We headed out to go north. We were wearing wellies, mountaineering waterproofs and open-necked cagoules. We didn't have any backup: no sat phone and no locater beacon. We did have a hefty dose of enthusiasm. Our first camp was not far from Kulusuk. If you hear a siren, it's a sign of a strong wind called a piteraq which can flatten tents and is very dangerous. It means that which attacks you in the local language. As soon as we had put the tents up, a siren sounded, and we looked at each other. It was a perfect evening, not a breath of wind, so we got a brew on. We found out later it was the siren at the airport that a plane was about to board.

We started heading up the fjord system and found an old U.S landing strip for refuelling planes that flew across the Atlantic during the second world war. Debris of old oil drums, buildings and trucks littered this otherwise pristine landscape. The sea ice was pretty dense, and we thought that this was normal. We had to get out and pull the kayaks across the sea ice. Not an easy task as the cockpit was tiny, and dragging oneself out was awkward. We then had to drag the boats, feeling the ice in front of us with the paddles to check it was thick enough to walk on. If either of us had gone in, it would have been bad news with the inappropriate kit we were wearing for any form of cold-water immersion.

We tried to camp in the sun with the long daylight hours, and we were pretty lucky. However, a few times, we were in the shade, and it was Baltic. We had to wear full insulated jackets.

The sea ice was pretty bad. We tried to get to the top of a peak to look further north, to see if

WAITING FOR THE SEA ICE TO CLEAR ON
OUR WAY HOME

there was a way to get through. Unfortunately, we had to deal with a glacier wearing wellies and a tow rope. Leo was never a mountaineer and called a halt to this ascent once we started to see the crevasses.

We tried to make our way through the ice, taking it, in turn, to follow the channels through the sea ice. Sometimes we could push small channels wider with our arms while sitting in the boat. Eventually, we couldn't justify this anymore and headed down another fjord less packed with ice.

We hadn't seen anybody for ten days when we came across another kayaker named Jon. He was a famous Danish kayaker who had paddled most of the coast in Greenland. Jon was a great guy. When he saw that we didn't have a gun, he told us that he had shot a bear just by our camp a few years ago. Jon had landed on an iceberg the same year to get a better look down the fjord and, returning, found a bear was between him and his kayak. Jon was so mad that he had left the gun in the kayak that he ran down, screaming at the bear. Jon said we should try that. I have not forgotten a gun since, as I reckoned, I wasn't grumpy enough yet.

We carried on down the fjord through the ice

THE BIG ICEBERG

LEO AND I AT THE END OF THE TRIP, NOTICE
LACK OF DRYSUITS BUT FASHIONABLE WELLIES

THE JOURNEY NOT THE DESTINATION

**LEO'S SHORT CUT TO THE TENTS
AFTER THE DANCE**

till we came across a small bay with a steel-hulled yacht in it. Nobody seemed to be about, and we kayaked to the shore, where we met the owner. A french man called Eric invited us on board. It was a luxury. We hadn't had a proper wash for over two weeks, and we were drinking lovely French coffee and pastries with Eric and some attractive French ladies. Twenty minutes later, we were back in the kayaks and paddled off. We had to pinch ourselves that it had happened.

We were now running short of time and still had to get back to Kulusuk to catch our flight. The open sea choked with sea ice. It left us stranded for a couple of days until we had a change of wind direction. Then we had a break and headed off to try to round the headlands and get back in time.

We got back with a day to spare and pitched

our tent. We decided to go into the town and found the only bar. It was open for one evening only, and the local Inuit ladies were going to line dance for the evening. As always, it was the usual mix of bizarre antics and friendly drunks.

Eventually, I decided to go back to the tent and left Leo there, still dancing. A shortcut involved passing close to all the chained-up huskies, and I took the long way back to the tent. I was never sure how long their chains were and thus the reach of their jaws. A few hours later, I heard the howling and snapping of the dogs and the cries of human pain. I realised Leo had decided to run the gauntlet and lost.

You will be pleased to note he survived, albeit with a few chunks taken out of him. It was the fastest sobering up routine he had ever had.

# CHAPTER EIGHT

# FUNDING

# "How do you set up an expedition, from something small scale to a significant undertaking?

The answer, in a nutshell, is that you choose a good team. The people you go with are far more important than the objective. It would be best if you had a balance of good company and the right skills.

Three is a good number. Three helps you feel safe, to share leads on pitches and provide company on climbing ledges. In kayaking, three people provide good backup and another person to help with rescues and towing. Ask yourself, could you spend like times cooped up in a tent with them? Aim to share a shelter for all three, promoting team bonding and sharing, albeit a little more cramped in the tent.

What about funding? Do you think you can get some? Everybody has to start somewhere. Most of my trips have started with a photo or a description of somewhere. If you want to make something happen, it will.

There are many organisations out there to encourage people to follow their dreams. The money is often not huge but can be enough to make it happen. If you can sacrifice time and effort to set up an expedition, I can assure you you won't be disappointed. I have put in many applications over the years and have attended many interviews. Even today, I still can't work out if I will get funding when I apply.

The Winston Churchill memorial trust set up to provide cash for UK citizens of 18-65 to follow their dreams. It has various categories to apply for every year, one always being an expedition of at least a month in length to a remote area.

Leo and I had an idea to try to Kayak to the Magnetic North Pole. I got together a good proposal and got an interview. In the meantime, I told Leo to put in an application as well. The Interview was in Kensington. On arrival, they give me the names of the interview panel. These were high ranking members of the establishment. An Air vice Marshall accompanied me to the room and told me not to

worry. I sat on a chair in front of the Panel, and we had a reasonably relaxed chat. However, I didn't impress them as I got a letter telling me I had been unsuccessful. That same day I got a phone message from Leo saying we were in the money; he had been successful. The rest of the tale is in another chapter.

The Welsh sports association used to have an expedition fund; sadly, this has gone lost in council cuts. The interviews were always in Cardiff, and I managed to lift down with my old PYB boss, Iain, on the interview panel. There were a few faces I knew; people applying for funding for climbing trips. One team looked a bit rough as they had been partying in Cardiff the night before.

I went in first. I only had a few photos of the peak in Peru we wanted to climb. I baulked this up with a few shots of locals and Lamas. In those days, it was a slide film. As I took the tray of slides out of the projector, my first slide must have stayed. It was a picture of the peak from a distance. The next

team of lads I knew, who had been partying, went in and came out looking a bit confused. So did the next group. Eventually, Iain came out holding my slide and told me to put it away as the other teams had been blagging about my transparency as the mountain they were attempting and the Panel had had enough. Ironically we got some funding. I'm not sure about the others.

The Mount Everest Foundation funding event held at the royal geographic club in London was a senior and well-known institution. All the applicants sat outside, waiting for a slot. I knew one of the applicants. He was wearing a neck brace; not a good look to get money! He told me he had injured himself wearing one of those inflatable Sumo wrestlers' suits in a fight at a stag do. He had managed to ram his head into the other wrestler's arse and tweaked his neck; I told him he might want to come up with another story for the Panel.

Another applicant came out looking

crestfallen; he told me we weren't allowed any slides, just maps and photos. When he described his objective in the Himalayas, one of the more senior Panels (who had his eyes closed) suddenly woke up and told the applicant somebody climbed the peak 30 years ago. He had been at the first ascent party!

Getting money out of equipment manufacturers is almost impossible, but you might get some gear. The modest sums of cash you might get from these organisations is often enough to pay for travel only. Beyond that, it is up to you to make it happen. A bit of commitment, and it will work with the outcome always uncertain. The funding organisations know this, and as long as you aim to provide a report, it is all that is all they ask.

The Arctic Club represents scientists and explorers who donate money to fund people to have adventures. They are particularly keen for young people to apply. They meet once a year at the Scott polar institute to look through applications to grant funding. They have various awards and the winners invited to attend the annual dinner and talk about their expedition. It's a great event. It is black tie and is full of fascinating and friendly people, mainly from the older generation. They are keen to get new blood to apply to keep the club going. For me, it is one of the high lights of the year.

There is funding often available for other sports, mainly competitive and medal-winning. It seems like an adventure, and outstanding British achievements in mountaineering, paddle sports, and caving seem to have to rely on private organisations' generosity. We have an exceptional record of success in the areas of adventure and exploration, and it is a pity this has not had the recognition it should have had.

On an expedition, you are thrown together with people for a short but intense period. You must trust and have faith that the people you go with will be competent, resilient and pleasant company in harsh environments. I am lucky to draw on a pool of outdoor people, and I aim to work and play. I have also been away with people I haven't known well, and nearly all my experiences have been positive. I have always tried avoiding saying things in the heat of the moment and have found laughter the best antidote to tough times. I have been away with some of the people I rarely see again and some I work with still. Beneath it all lies the bond we get from pushing ourselves in remote areas and situations away from everyday life.

# CHAPTER
## NINE

# ALASKA AND THE PIOLET D'OR

THE JOURNEY NOT THE DESTINATION

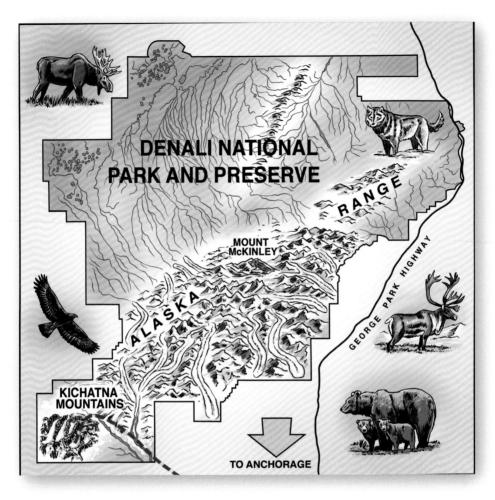

DENALI NATIONAL PARK

END OF DAY THREE,
NEAR THE SUMMIT

**KICHATNA MOUNTAINS**

Autumn 2003, going into the staff room at Plas Y Brenin, Louise Thomas, our Chief Instructor, stops me. Then tells me that our recent Alaskan expedition nominated for The Piolet d'Or. I had no idea what this was, but she explained it was like the Oscars for climbing. We had to go to Grenoble to present our trip to a Panel of Esteemed climbers, who would decide who would get the Golden Ice Axe for a significant new climb.

All expenses paid a meal, and a good piss-up with fellow climbers sounded great.

We are Flying into Kitchatna Spires Area with Paul from Kalteekna Air Taxi in the plane is Mike Twid Turner and Stu Mcleese. Both had been into this area before and had eyes on a few objectives. I had been to Patagonia in 92 with Twid and had a

great time, but it was the first time away with Stu. The pair had climbed together before, with Twid being Stu's mentor figure, so although he was a great climber Twid was the more substantial part of the relationship. I had come through the Instructional Apprenticeship schemes with Twid, so I think I balanced our team structure.

The landscape beneath the plane was mainly Tundra and Forrest. Paul, the pilot, usually flew to People to climb Denali, Alaska's highest peak. He said it was a nice break to fly to Kitchatna. The heights of Kitchatna came into view, and it seemed immense. We flew in this circle of mountains, and it felt like a giant door shutting behind capturing in this magical place. Paul banked the plane. We started to descend to the Shadows Glacier.

It looked like a massive open runway deposited on all sides by peaks. The landing was so soft we hardly felt it. We unloaded, and in no time, the plane was a distant speck in the distance, and silence surrounded us.

The following morning, we headed up to a col that overlooked the next valley and one of our Middle triple East peak objectives. The terrain crevassed, but eventually, we reached the col with the wind adding a bit of spice to the view. I looked across to the objective; it seemed miles away. We would have to negotiate the ground we had just come up and get over to the peak with lots of gear. It seemed a big job before we even started climbing and exposing ourselves to risk. I looked down from the col towards our tent. It looked like a tiny speck on the vast Shadows glacier.

That night in the tent, I suggested we went for the Ice gully we had been looking at from the camp on Kitchatna spires. I think we all agreed this was sensible and nearby with no hidden difficulties to get to the start of it. It looked like a fantastic line, narrow gully splitting the mountain, with ice and snow all the way; it looked steep and narrow 1000m metres of climbing.

The sun was coming up over the mountains as we reached the base of the climb, golden fingers of light bathing the cliff above while we were still in the cold below. We started climbing, swapping leads; the first pitches involved slabby rocky technical slopes, followed by steep ice pitches. We established ourselves in the gully proper. We abseiled down, leaving a fixed rope in place.

The idea was now to carry a large haul bag with bivy gear and go for it the following day. We had 50m climbing ropes and a 100m low stretch rope. One person would lead the second to follow and drag the fixed-line. the third then ascend that fixed-line while the lead climber did the next pitch and then repeat the process; we had no real idea how long we would be on the mountain

We swapped leads and continued up the gully all that day; it got so narrow you could touch the sides. Unfortunately meant that it became a shooting gallery with the ice knocked down came straight down on anybody below. Late that afternoon, I got hit by a block of ice on the shoulder, ice is very heavy for its size, and it knocked the wind out of me. I screamed out and slowly caught my breath; Twid was next to me. We started to work out damage, I couldn't move my arm above my shoulder, but I didn't think I had broken anything. Stu had sorted out the First aid. To say it was minimalist would be generous, a triangular bandage and a few wound dressings, no pain killers or drugs.

We carried on. I was able to ascend the ropes using jumars and a foot loop. We reached a Forty-degree triangular ice patch; we had noticed from the ground about halfway up the mountain.

We started to dig using our axes, and after an hour, we had created tiny flat coffins we could lie flat in. At that point, an avalanche of spindrift snow came down the gully, we had not had any this all day, and it filled up the coffins and buried up to our knees. We were too tired and had nowhere else to go, so we dug out our sleeping area, had a brew and got into our sleeping bags. It was a restless night, cold bright, the stars twinkling through the

gully. I couldn't sleep or find a position that didn't hurt my shoulder and counted the hours till dawn.

Stu looked like shit, and Twid got a brew on; above us lay a steep I pitch which Twid led and fixed a rope, the ice was bullet hard, and stuff was flying around glinting as it bounced down the gully. We had been placing bolts, hammering into granite with a handheld driver and an ice axe. It took about 40 mins, and as I was not leading anymore because of the shoulder, I did all the hauling and bolt placing. After the last bolt, I had now sheared all the pins holding the axe together and now only had one axe.

Stu and Twid were doing an excellent job on the lead, but we were still getting hit by ice, we used the haul bag as protection, and every once in a while, the bag would shudder as a big lump hit it. It's a bloody shooting gallery and nowhere to hide. I said to Stu that somebody would get badly hurt soon.

Finally, we ended up in an ice cave; it felt like a protective haven, a chance to gather breath and focus on the final push. At last, the angle eased, and we pushed on up the final slopes to a col between the summits, at last rewarded with views of surrounding mountains after the claustrophobic atmosphere of the gully.

The sun was slowly setting, and we reached the summit, and it looked like the surrounding mountains were on fire with the setting sun. The aim had been to Bivy on the summit as we had been going non-stop for a few days. But alongside the sun's orange glow were ominous clouds coming in. We decided reluctantly to head down. We were tired. But the thought of retreating in an Alaskan storm gave us a new impetus.

**STU ON THE LONG ABSEIL RETREAT
DURING THE NIGHT**

**DIGGING THE COFFINS TO
SLEEP IN - END OF DAY 2**

We decided that as we had two 50m rope and 100m of static rope, the first two would abseil down on the 100m. The last man would tie the two 50m together and connect that to the 100m and come down with somebody below holding onto the two 50m to counterbalance the last down. It meant we could retrieve the ropes and do a considerable distance each time.

It all sounds complicated; it worked but had a few flaws if somebody wasn't holding the 50m ropes. Catastrophe, in the dark with the storm starting and communication difficult, so we took our time. We also got away with all the rope, not getting caught on retrieval because the gully was smooth and steep. We carried this slow process all night, small avalanches pouring down on top of us.

Twid had Relieved himself on the Bivy on the way up. As we descended in the dark past this point, we find remnants of his poo, now frozen solid for hundreds of meters. Stu reckoned we could abseil

of it and said it must have been like a Mr whippy ice cream van tap left on!

We were eventually spat out of the gully, like peas in a pod in the early hours of the morning. We dragged ourselves and the mass of rope slowly back to the tent, had a brew and collapsed asleep.

The storm raged for a few days dumping inches of snow on the mountains and the glacier; we slept, ate and dug our tent out. A Polish team was stuck on a wall in porta-ledges; we located their tent eventually on the glacier. We dug it out for them, for when they managed to get down. Avalanches were going off all around, and we realised that was it for anymore climbing for a while

Twid got on the sat phone and got hold of Paul to come and retrieve us when he could; instead, we would be sitting in Talkeetna instead of freezing on the glacier. Eventually, it stopped snowing and using our snowshoes, we stamped up an down for hours, creating a landing strip and then marked this out with bags of snow.

**TWID ENJOYING THE SUMMIT AS THE STORM CLOUDS ARE ROLLING IN**

At last, we heard the noise of a plane, we pulled down the tent, and all the rest of our bags were ready. Slowly Paul descended, landed and then gave us a massive bollocking about the airstrip and how lazy we were. He eventually calmed down, and we got in, and he gave it full throttle and got us up. Away, the conversation limited on the way home, but we arrived back in Talkeetna late afternoon.

A quick shower and we hit the town, albeit one main bar. The call Talkeetna a small drinking town with a climbing problem. They must see many climbers back from there adventures, some successful, some not, but all are gagging for a drink; we were no exception. We started on beers, then ordered Tequila, the bar lady asked for cash, and Stu gave her a $100 bill and said, let us know when that runs out. The nights a bit of a blur, but I do remember going outside with a beer and coming across the Bar lady smoking a massive joint; she offered me a puff but also said it was illegal to drink my beer in the street and also told me we had run out of credit

What about the Piolet d'Or? Did we win?

No, a Russian team did for an Alpine-style climb on an 8000m peak, very impressive. Anyway, the whole idea of Mountaineering first ascents being part of a competition is strange. None of us climbs to win awards, and we climb to experience the challenge, environment and good company. It was never about the destination for me but the journey. I can apply wholeheartedly to the objective when we arrive, but failure rates can be high because of the environment. Anyway, now all the teams get the award, there is no overall winner if you get nominated. Everybody gets recognised, Far better and a good excuse for a celebration of achievements and a party.

Looking back, our Team worked well; we all knew each other from work. Twid was the driving force as usual, and Stu a robust and talented climber; I was there for the balance, I think. We all came back alive, stayed friends and had a lot of laughs. What more could you ask?

Being comfortable
about being
uncomfortable

# THE HIGH MOUNTAINS

# "It is all about that journey, not the destination;

I read on the back of an aircraft's headrest advertising a car hire company. Its 2000 and We were heading to India to the big mountains. There were three of us, Iain, Martin and myself. I was the team leader; the others told me when we had to deal with any officials, which for anybody that knows Indian bureaucracy means a lot.

The only reason I qualified for this role is I had come up with the idea to climb in The Parabati area in the Northern Indian state of Himachal Pradesh and managed to get some funding sorted.

We met Mohan, our agent from Kash Travel, and he led us through the madness of Delhi to our hotel. When I told him we had to pick up a barrel of gear we had shipped, his face dropped. Why didn't you tell me before he said, and I could have told you to pay for excess baggage instead? I will be here to pick you, meaning me, early tomorrow morning to try and sort this out.

The next day I was introduced to the complexity and rituals of Indian bureaucracy, inherited from us the British Mohan was keen to point out. We spent all day going from office to office, shaking hands, filling in documents and paying what looked like large sums of cash across. I passed fire exit stairs blocked with masses of paper files and the clatter of old typewriters filling the air. Eventually, we had the proper paperwork, and we headed to Airport Cargo. After all the money that had passed hands, I asked Mohan how much we owed him, about twenty dollars. He told me with

a smile, but we have another problem: the whole country shuts down in an hour for four days for a religious festival.

We reached the massive storage facility gates, and I could see our small Barrell down the end. Mohan was flashing paperwork at an official; with little joy, I could see one of the workers next to it, so I whistled, pointed to Barrell and waved a five-dollar bill. Miraculously the barrel appeared, the money given, and two minutes later, the doors shut down for a holiday; Mohan told me I was getting the hang of how it worked here in India but then said Five dollars was a little steep.

When you climb in India, you have to obtain a permit from the Indian mountain federation and allocated a liaison officer to check you are climbing the correct peak. Anil was our liaison officer who we had to kit out, and he came with us to the start of our trek into Parvati. The valley is full of marijuana plants, and a lot of hippys live there getting stoned. I saw Martin casually grab a handful, and I tried discreetly to grab some, but a porter saw me. He grinned, showing his one right tooth. We never did get to smoke it, we wanted to dry it out away from camp, but we didn't have any papers or pipe, so we gave up, never had Cannabis so surrounded me; I am sure the porters were on it. They butchered a sheep one night. All I saw was a severed head at first, and they hacked it up on a plastic sheet; how none of them lost their toes, I have no idea. There was another team in the camping area, and the

NICK UNDER THE NORTH FACE
OF CHANGABANG AT 5000M,
INDIAN HIMALAYAS

**BIVY ON PARBATTI IN INDIAN HIMALAYAS
AT 6000M**

leader came across and asked who were are porters. Nepalese, I replied. These men are savages, he said and walked off.

They may have lacked butchery skills, but having worked with Nepalese before, they were hard as nails and would not let you down.

We reached base camp and set off to the mountain. Our first camp was on the glacier. We found a large boulder and camped on top of it, and we had to remind ourselves of this when we got up for a pee. Parbati looked impressive from here. Rob, a friend of ours, had done the first ascent but said the west ridge was unclimbed and looked inviting.

The following day we got on it; I climbed a series of corner systems to get on the ridge, you had to be very careful with the large loose blocks, and with a rucksack of bivy gear and the altitude, it was hard going.

THE JOURNEY NOT THE DESTINATION

**THE APPROACH COULOIR ON WEST FACE
OF CHANGABANG**

Eventually, all of us ended up on the ridge and slept on a small ledge; the scenery was impressive with the clouds rolling up the valley. We pushed on the following day but encountered more and more loose rock, and eventually, we retreated. We had run out of time and trekked out to the town of Bhuntar to pick up our transport back to Delhi. Our cooks prepared us the last meal, and we went sent out for a few beers, now. As it is supposedly a dry state, you have to buy them sneakily, and they are super strong. The evening progressed, and Iain got out the Whisky; he had a knack of pretending to swig it but taking in very little; I was gulping it back by this time. I don't remember going to bed, but I. do remember waking up in the early hours feeling awful and looking for the paracetamol. unfortunately, we had inherited an old friend's first aid kit, which consisted of mainly veterinary stuff as it was cheaper and all in film capsules.

When morning eventually came, I realised I had taken antibiotics for chest wounds for horses washed down with local tap water. The two-day journey back to Delhi resulted in a massive weight loss due to it coming out of both ends of my body. The Final insult was going to the Imperial Hotel in Delhi, a leftover from the British Raj with its fantastic architecture and food, watching Iain and Martin tuck into a feast. At the same time, I could only manage a weak vegetable broth.

Changabang, the Shining mountain, was in the Garwhal Himalaya of Uttarakhand in India near the Chinese border, and it was almost 7000m high. It was a mountain I had read about and inspired by Pete Boardman's book on the first ascent of the West face, something that had been unrepeated.

Nick and Stu had funding for a trip to the mountain, and another pair had dropped out. I had climbed with Stu in Alaska in another chapter. Nick was a full-time climber and very talented. I knew him from instructing him on a climbing course years before and being involved in his winter mountain leader assessment.

I would already be in India on a trekking holiday with my partner Lissie, and we would meet up at the end of my trip. Stu and Nick turned up at the 5-star hotel we were staying at, looking like a pair of tramps. They had been staying as some cheap dive in the city., an indication of the trip ahead.

We had our Indian army liaison officer with us and Raja, our tour operator and his head guide. We drove all day to eventually land up in Hardiwar, where all the pilgrims had gathered for the annual Kanwar Mela. The city was full of life, and when we came down for supper, we found three plastic chairs and a table laid out in an empty, soulless room in our boarding lodge. We all decided to get out of here and into the city and had a fantastic evening wandering around. When we got back, our Liason officer had called the police and Nick as our leader, carted off for questioning. One phone call to the Indian mountaineering federation, and he was back with the liaison officer suitably reprimanded, and now we had as little to do with him as possible.

One more journey to Josimoouth, and we were trekking into our base camp.

There was another team there from Holland trying to climb the North Face, and amused at our mountain tents our company had provided; they looked like cheap supermarket tents. I was not impressed either.

The Bergini glacier lay in front, and we started carrying loads up through this maze, picking our way through the glacial debris and putting stone cairns in to mark the way. We set up a series of camps before the final one on a very uneven small patch of rough ground.

According to the Dutch, the weather had been excellent, and the following morning we started climbing, aiming to head to a col on the west face. It was hard at around 6000m, but Nick and I climbed hard ice towards some rocky areas. Nick left the gully of good ice and headed for the rock band. When I arrived to look at some belay built-in dodgy rock, I asked him why he had belayed here, he said I know you, Instructors, like a good rock belay. I replied I did, but this wasn't and introduced him to an Ice thread belay made with ice screws.

We used this method for hauling and ascending the ropes over the next few days, moving the kit up to the col. On the first ascent, the climbers came in from the valley on the other side, which was a considerably easier approach, but this was now closed to climbers.

The Dutch were making steady progress, and so were we. I was running short of time and wished I could extend my flight but had no way of doing this. The dutch asked me if I would like to use their pigeon, which I discovered was their code word for satphone. They were not supposed to have one in this sensitive area, so I phoned out and changed my flight.

That seemed to be the signal for it all to go wrong, as that evening it started to snow and didn't stop for days. I was getting out every 3 hours to dig our tent out. Some of the dutch climbers were still on the mountain, and we could hear avalanches going off regularly. The other dutch climbers and I went looking for them, visibility was abysmal, and we waded through waist-deep snow, but eventually, the staggered out of the gloom with the stare of men who knew how lucky they were to be alive.

The next day we all started to head down, the dutch were going home, and we were leaving our tent hopefully to return. The next ten hours seemed the most exhausting I had done. The glacier-covered in the snow with the possibility of falling into a hole and breaking something was a constant fear. we had to try and find our original markers in the snow and mist, but eventually, we all collapsed into base camp.

We slept and recovered in the mess tent, eating and sleeping while it still snowed. It would take days

**CHANGABANG**

to settle and be safe to attempt going up, and I had now resigned myself to heading out. I had been to India for months and had to get back now. I realised even though I had extended my flight a little, I didn't have the timescale left to deal with the weather that had hit us. Nick and Stu still had the right amount of time, and it was with very mixed emotions I left.

All the hard work of ferrying gear and being at the point that we had made it to the main climbing. The thoughts of leaving the team worrying, about the conditions they would now face, The mountains once again had changed the odds so quickly against us.

The high mountains are all about suffering from a slim success rate, with so many factors against you, weather, altitude and sickness. For me, although they were stunning places involving commitment and time, I felt that my time in this environment was over. Many other mountains gave you more of a chance of success and journies on the sea. I wouldn't have swapped my time attempting Himalayan climbing and being humbled by the high mountains.

# CHAPTER
## ELEVEN

# AN OLD FART AND YOUNG AND BUCKS

THE ROUTE AROUND MILNE ISLAND

Youth is wasted
on the young
*Oscar Wilde*

BEN PADDLING AMONG THE ICEBERGS

# "Going away with the right people is fundamental to whether or not an expedition will be enjoyable.

**THE UNTOUCHABLES**

Going away with the right people is fundamental to whether or not an expedition will be enjoyable. I used to have three basic rules; come back alive, stay friends with the people you go with and, finally, have a fun time. Humour can disperse most problems. Success in the objective is a bonus. I am not saying you don't try hard to achieve the goal, but if any of the three rules are severely compromised, I don't think it's worth it.

Finding a balance between motivation and common sense is the key. It's good to have youthful enthusiasm, mixed with a good bit of old sweats experience and wisdom.

With all this in mind, I went about planning a trip to N.E Greenland. We would be going into the most extensive fjord system in the world; Scorsbysund. I had asked Ben to come, he was a work colleague and housemate, and I had mentored him as a young instructor. Ben suggested the third member; Dan, an old school friend of Ben's, and I knew him vaguely. Both were competent climbers

and paddlers. I was pretty sure they would be good company, despite this being their first big expedition.

Dan went after Winston Churchill memorial trust funding and got some. I got some welsh sports association money, so we were off. The idea was to explore Milne Island at the bottom of Scorsbysund and attempt new Alpine-style climbs.

We shipped the kayaks, generously donated by our Sponsor Palm, and two barrels of kit. We had to hope they would arrive. The gear goes by the arctic line, which supplies all the small communities. On the East Coast of Greenland, there is Ammasilak and then nothing for about 2000 km, till you get to the small settlement of Ittoqqoormit that had around 400 souls.

We flew to Iceland, Then onto Constable point, which had a gravel strip airstrip on a river delta west of the settlement. We then had, Then a short helicopter ride to Itiqutormit. As we took off, Ben had the passenger seat at the front, "fast and

**ICEBERGS!**

low", he said to the pilot. The stern-looking Danish pilot looked at him and said, "high and slow", but even that gave us fantastic views.

Anna, a Belgian girl, who was here to race huskies met us. She took us to our accommodation - basically a shipping container with windows, doors and a bed. The next day we went in search of our equipment.

Nannu travel had taken possession of the kit from the cargo boats, and we popped in to see them. Martin and Karina ran this business. Martin was an ex Danish Sirius patrol member, and he had a steely-eyed and direct approach. Karina was bubbly and friendly. We had arranged with Martin to get dropped off at Milne island, and we had assumed the price of £1000 was for a pickup as well. It was not the case, and as we didn't have any more money, we told him just to drop us off. He looked surprised and told us it was a long way to paddle back. He shrugged and said maybe he would see us and perhaps not.

Dragged out of our beds at 2 am to start the journey, we loaded the kayaks and sped off down the Fjord. The driver was skimming in and out around the icebergs at high speed. We dozed, slumped over the kayaks. After 5 hours, we arrived at the east end of Milne Island by an old wireless station. There was another mountaineering team waiting for a pickup. Double bubble for Martin, we thought as we unloaded the kayaks and the barrels and went to check out the hut.

Milne Island is a large island around 300km in circumference. We had food for 27 days, plus all the camping and climbing gear in the three kayaks. We were lucky the boats were a generous size, but we still had lots of kit rammed into the cockpit area. We weren't getting out in a hurry if we capsized.

We headed down the south side of the Island, looking for climbing possibilities. We spent a day exploring a valley that looked promising, but most of the climbs seemed too steep. On our way back, the valley was blocked by a herd of Musk Ox, giant

**DAN AND BEN NORTH SIDE OF MILNE ISLAND**

shaggy bison, and you had to watch out for the males. Martin told us a male charged him, and he let it have it at close range to the head with a solid lead slug. Their skulls are so thick that this didn't kill them. It shook its head and wandered off, and started grazing.

Unfortunately, the gun he had given us looked like it was for a bank hold up with a short barrel and pistol grip handle. Our attempts at practising resulted in being blown back off our feet and no hits on the target. We hoped the noise would scare anything away.

Eventually, at the eastern end of the Island, we came across a mountain called Hergenlitop. It looked like it had potential, so we headed off the following day. We had 1000FT of good climbing and a long day with the main hazard being the loose rock and peregrines dive-bombing us halfway up. We called the Climb the Sleeping Giant due to the profile of the mountain from the sea kayaks. We graded it XS 5b, a mountain grade taking in to account the loose rock.

On the way down, we started to see our camp and kayaks. On closer inspection, I could only count two. There is only a tiny tide in the Fjord, and the

boys insisted it couldn't be theirs missing, as they had tied their boats to the shore so any wave coming could not have washed them off. I, on the other hand, realised that I hadn't.

I thought of all the parameters as we got close; we had no sat phone or any communication with the outside world.

We had a few options. The boys could paddle back to Ittoqqortoormiit, a journey of 9 days, and send a boat for me. In the meantime, I could take enough food and walk back to the old wireless Hut across the mountains.

Before all this, Ben and I headed out in the remaining kayaks to look for mine. Luckily there had been no wind that day, and we found it tucked into a small inlet about 2km away. Everything was sitting there with my cockpit open. It could have disappeared anywhere, and it would have scuppered us. Needless to say, while before the boys had taken my words like gospel from an old seasoned expeditioner, I was now largely ignored.

We soon headed down the North coast and had a fantastic encounter with a pod of Narwhale. They have a formidable spear-like tusk emanating from their foreheads. The locals hunted these shy

**DAN ON TOP PITCH OF THE SLEEPING GIANT XS 5B**

and rare creatures, and their yellow blubber was considered a delicacy. The local hunters asked if we had seen any when we finished the trip, and we suddenly had memory loss.

The Northside of the Island was stunning with granite spires. These were all primary climbing objectives, but we didn't have the kit or the time for these challenges, as we had a long paddle home.

We arrived at the North Coast end of the bear islands, an unfortunate name considering our firepower. We found evidence of a bear kill near an old disused hut, bear claws and skin. After a rest day, we prepared for the long stretch of Jameson Land.

We were running low on food, and the weather was turning colder and wetter. We had also broken our primary stove, so we had to cook on fires from wood scavenged from the shore. We ran out of our main food supply due to the extra paddling days and survived on the scraps we had left. We all had significant weight loss due to the long paddling days but felt good we just dreamt

of food all the time. Happily, a couple of days later, we arrived back at the settlement. We had made a journey of over 500km and done a new mountain route. Importantly, we had complied with all three of my rules for a successful expedition.

As we paddled in, there was a fantastic wooden boat moored up. As we landed, a bearded gentleman came up to us and asked us how long we had been out. He invited us for a meal that evening. His crew came and got us later. We found out he was Arvid Fuchs, a famous explorer. He told us that his team had wintered over in this spot before, and they almost didn't get out of the Fjord the following year.

Wintering over wasn't for us, and the next day we were back on the helicopter, this time with a different pilot. Ben asked again, "fast and low", the pilot looked at him and said, "Is there any other way?". He lifted the aircraft off the pad and flew low level; to our screams from the back, "You stupid bastard Ben".

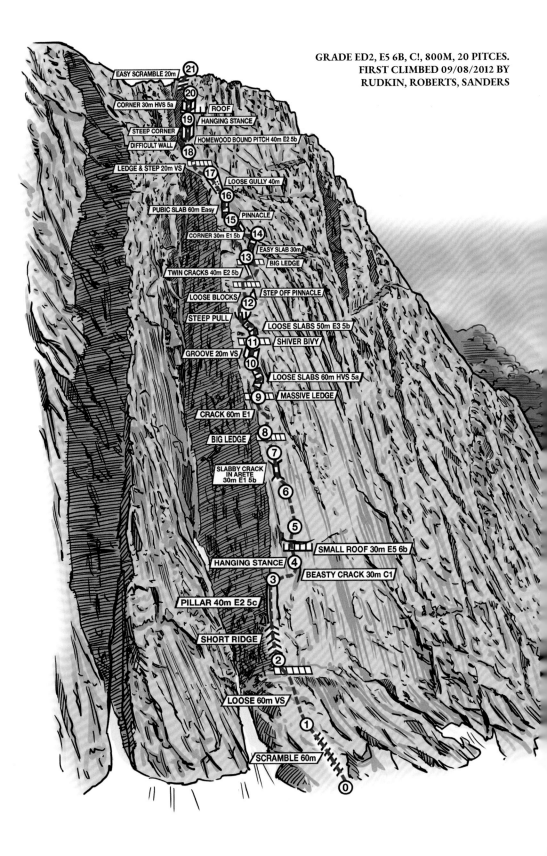

GRADE ED2, E5 6B, C!, 800M, 20 PITCES.
FIRST CLIMBED 09/08/2012 BY
RUDKIN, ROBERTS, SANDERS

EASY SCRAMBLE 20m — 21

20

CORNER 30m HVS 5a — ROOF — 19
STEEP CORNER — HANGING STANCE
DIFFICULT WALL — HOMEWOOD BOUND PITCH 40m E2 5b — 18
LEDGE & STEP 20m VS — 17
LOOSE GULLY 40m — 16
PUBIC SLAB 60m Easy — 15 — PINNACLE
CORNER 30m E1 5b — 14
13 — EASY SLAB 30m
BIG LEDGE
TWIN CRACKS 40m E2 5b
LOOSE BLOCKS — STEP OFF PINNACLE
12
STEEP PULL
LOOSE SLABS 50m E3 5b
11 — SHIVER BIVY
GROOVE 20m VS — 10
LOOSE SLABS 60m HVS 5a
9 — MASSIVE LEDGE
CRACK 60m E1
8 — BIG LEDGE
7
SLABBY CRACK
IN ARETE
30m E1 5b — 6
5
SMALL ROOF 30m E5 6b
HANGING STANCE — 4
BEASTY CRACK 30m C1
3
PILLAR 40m E2 5c
SHORT RIDGE
2
LOOSE 60m VS
1
SCRAMBLE 60m
0

# CHAPTER
## TWELVE

# DROWNING IN A SEA OF LIGHT

# "It was July 2010, and I had spent a long time staring at the large rock face

at the end of the Fjord we had camped at for a few days. We were on the south side of Qaersorssuaq island, a mostly uninhabited island in N.W Greenland. I was here on a month's kayaking and climbing trip with Sid and Nigel.

We had been climbing new multi-pitch routes up to E2 grade. The climb at the end of the Fjord looked too big and too hard for us. The campsite was idyllic. It had loads of wood and fresh water in a stunning location. The image of that unclimbed rock face burnt a picture in my mind, and I knew

I would be back.

It took a couple of years to find the right team and get funding. The Arctic and Alpine Club helped with funding, and we were on our way. A flight to Copenhagen, then another the following day to Kangerlussuaq. We then had a smaller prop plane and an overnight, followed by yet another short hop on a twin-prop plane. Finally, we were on the island of Upernavik, with a small population of about 500 souls. With an 800m runway, the airport had been made by levelling the island's high point.

**UPERNAVIK FROM THE AIR**

From here, we walked down to our local contact Nicloaj. By we, I mean Dave, Lee and myself. I worked with Dave and Lee, and they were both excellent climbers and, as important, good company.

However, Lee and Dave were not kayakers, so we arranged a drop-off and pick up from Upernavik. Our kit was late arriving, and we had to wait a few days. We had shipped out most of the food and all the climbing gear, including a porta ledge. With this, we could hang off a sheer rock face and sleep.

We got the gear, loaded it onto a small boat we had organised, and headed out. The local guide started heading out to the open sea rather than go the more sheltered route, and I got the map out again. We carried on, and we were looking at the fuel, and it was getting low. At last, we got off the rough ocean and arrived in the Fjord. We were

concerned he wouldn't get back, but he produced more fuel from a secret compartment. We paid him half the fee, and he promised to come back in a month. As we saw him disappear, we realised how quiet it was and how alone we were on this island.

The beach we camped on was stunning, apart from the plastic. So while we were settling in and sorting gear, we cleared as much plastic as possible of the beach. We had a play with the gun, and it became apparent that it was faulty; it went off as we were operating the bolt to put a bullet in the barrel: luckily, nobody was hurt. We had to load it very carefully, but only with one shot. We hoped we would never have to use it.

We spent a few days exploring the area and climbed some new routes not far from the camp. We called Heroes of Hotness an excellent E2 five-pitch

**LEE AND DAVE HALWAY UP UP THE ROUTE
AFTER THE STORM**

route and blessed with an easy descent back to camp.

The next day we packed up the climbing gear and walked down the Fjord's side to the main event, our trip up the big rock face. What would have taken me half an hour in a kayak took us a couple of hours due to the boulder fields we had to weave through. We got to the base of the pillar. After some easy climbing, Dave set off to the top of the pillar at the route's start. We all eventually ended up sitting on top of it in the evening light.

The next pitch looked hard, and Lee stated aid climbing up it. It would go free but harder than any of us could climb. With magnificent views of the calm glass-like Fjord onward to the open sea, Dave and I watched him. Lee finished and left a fixed line in place; we decided to head down and back to camp. It was ten o'clock in the evening, and

we had got established on the climb.

The next time we came back, we carried a haul bag. A heavy-duty pack with various straps that you use to haul it up the climb contains food, water, waterproof clothing and other essentials.

The idea was we could keep climbing as it didn't get dark. We ascended to our last point and then started climbing. The climbing was good, and Dave led the hard pitches. I hauled the bag on stances. It went well at first as the climbing was very steep. After a while, the angle eased a little, and the haul bag kept getting caught, but we carried on, and we were making good progress. The sky was darkening with clouds. We hadn't got a Sat Phone or any way of getting a forecast. We were on a small ledge system 400m up the climb when the storm came in. all we had were our waterproofs: we had

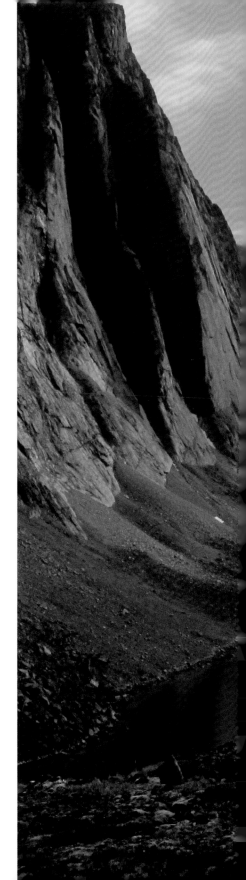

no sleeping bags or shelter. We settled in best we could, and we dozed on and off for hours. It was very windy, and I could see the wind creating white caps on the sea below. The rain increased. We had no idea how long the storm would last. It would take a day or so for the rock to dry, and we were getting wet and cold, so we had to go down.

We damaged the rope over a sharp edge on the first abseil, so we isolated this with a knot then carried on descending. It took us all night, careful not to damage the ropes and avoid knocking rocks on those below. The storm blew, and the rain continued. Semi hypothermic, we arrived on the ground. We then had two hours of boulder hopping on the wet, greasy rock. Exhausted, we got back to camp and got a brew on.

We spent the next few days sleeping and eating. Eventually, the weather started to clear. We had no way of knowing if this would last, so we did the walk along the shore back to the base of the climb and ascended some of the ropes we had left, hoping they hadn't suffered damage in the storm. This time we went super light, and we eventually reached our previous high point and just kept climbing. We didn't need to worry about the

**LEE AIDING THE PITCH FROM
THE PILLAR**

daylight as it never got dark. The final pitches were fantastic, E2 climbing on good rock and eventually, we all pulled over on top of the plateau.

We found a pair of antlers on the summit. How old were these: hundreds or thousands of years when the icecap covered the land? We had a fantastic walk over with the fingers of golden light warming us and enticing us back to our camp.

We had a few days left, and we hoped the boat would come for us. The Boatman caught us off guard early in the morning, and we rushed to take the tent down as we heard the noise of his engine in the distance coming down the Fjord.

Our flight was in three days, and luckily there was a once a year football tournament on a gravel pitch. The ball was being frequently kicked into the sea and retrieved. It did mean that the bar and small village hall was open for one night.

Nikolaj warned us to be careful as he worked at the health clinic and did all the STD tests. I don't know if he thought we were all sex-starved from our month's adventure. All we wanted was to drink beer. It was the usual affair of cheesy music and only beer, no spirits. All the local men just sat and drank, which meant the wives dragged us on the dance floor most of the night. The local ladies had hands everywhere, but it was a great evening.

Nikolaj made us steak and chips for our last

night: although the meat was a little weird. He eventually owned up and told us it was polar Bear, the one-shot rampaging in the village. We were glad to be leaving and walked to the airport at the top of the town.

We called the route Drowning in a Sea of Light due to the storm and daylight hours. It wasn't the team's first choice of name. Lee and Dave had bought a men's magazine. On the cover were generously chested models dressed as superheroes. They had the title 'Heroes of Hotness'. A name they want for our climb. I was having none of that as I thought it deserved a bit more gravitas. They completely surprised me when they came back with 'drowning in a sea of light'. Perfect and summed up the great adventure we had just had.

CHAPTER
# TWELVE

# OPEN CROSSINGS

THE JOURNEY NOT THE DESTINATION

Nae man can
tether time
nor tide
*Rabbie Burns
Tam o' Shanter*

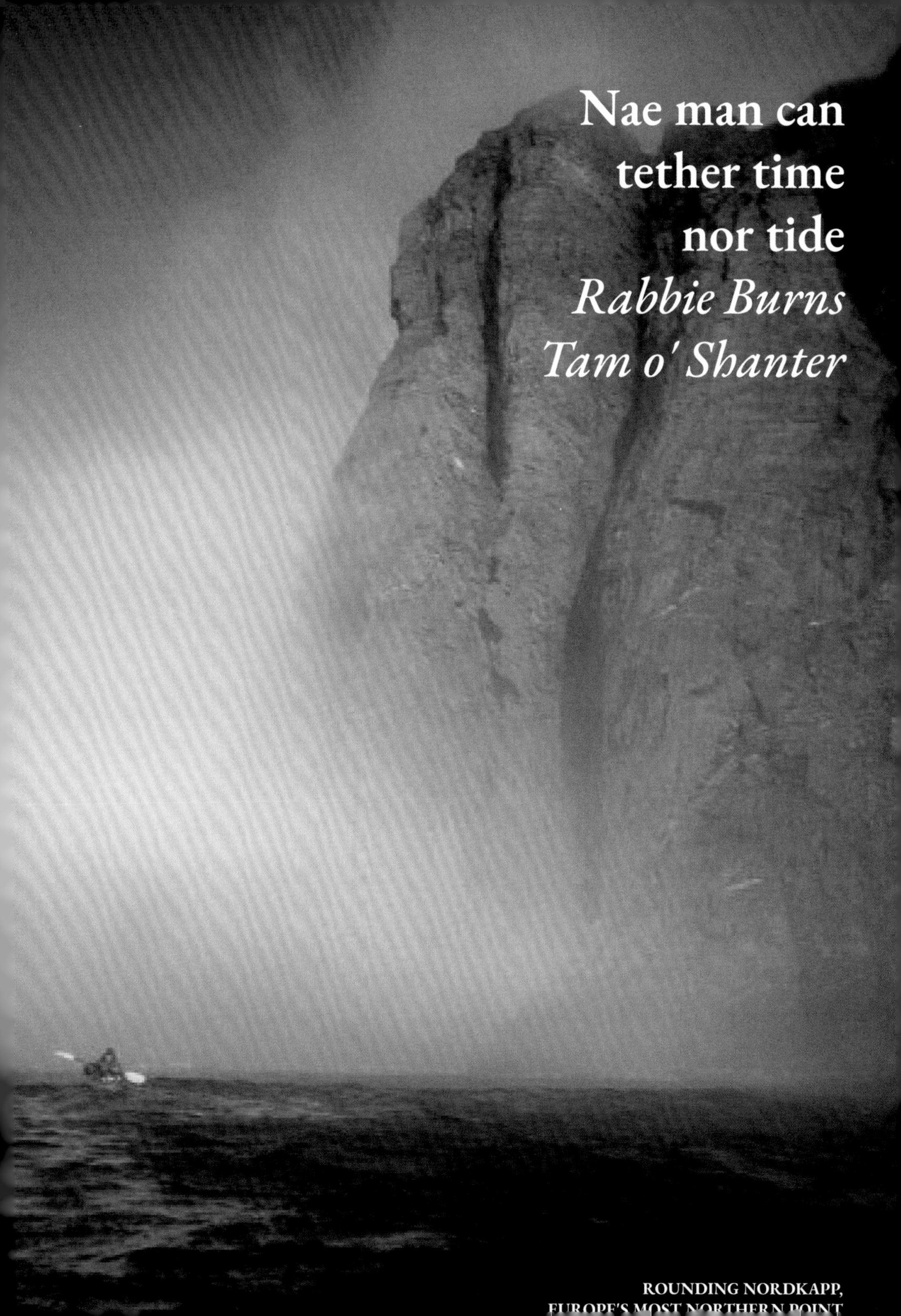

ROUNDING NORDKAPP,
EUROPE'S MOST NORTHERN POINT

# ""We're in the money" was all the phone message said from Leo.

I had applied for funding for a trip to Kayak to magnetic North. For me, it was a relatively well thought out application. I had told Leo to apply as well, although I had left where up to him.

"We are going to Kayak from Scotland to Russia," he told me later. The criteria for this, he said, was that he had opened an atlas, and this seemed like a good idea.

We had both applied to the Winston Churchill Memorial Trust Fund. Winston Churchill had set this up to enable Uk citizens to go on adventures or pursue projects that would benefit them and the community.

If you get an interview, you must go to London and have a chat with a board of eminent public figures, who change most years. You sit in a leather chair facing them and have a conversation. Having been involved in the process, the more outrageous and poorly planned and bonkers your idea is, and if you come across as keen, you get some funding. Exactly how Leo fits in, so that was it; we

were going from Shetland across the North Sea and all the way along the Norwegian coast to Russia.

Significant open sea crossings in a kayak are a step-change in any kayaker's development. Being alone in a considerable area of the sea for many hours, relying on navigation, boat handling, seamanship, and endurance is a real test in any small craft and particularly one you are under your power.

Leo and I had worked together at PYB for many years running Scottish and Irish sea kayaking expeditions. We had built up a good working relationship. We both had experience looking after people and our groups, and we had many memorable and funny adventures.

For example, we had crossed the Irish Sea, from Holyhead to Dun Laoghaire, in a double sea kayak. It took 18 hours and had been a poorly planned last-minute adventure. We had managed to persuade Dave Torrington, head of Kayaking at Plas Menai, to lend us a double kayak; we told Dave that we were going for a paddle around the coast.

We left Holyhead on Anglesey at around 2 pm to get a favourable tide and headed around North Stack and then out to the west. We called the coastguard and told them of our plans. Unfortunately, that was the last time the radio worked. We couldn't work out how to use the GPS as neither of us had read the instructions. Still, we both figured it's a big target if we keep heading west. We paddled into the sunset, feeling very alone in a big sea. We got into a rhythm; 2 hours paddling, then 5 mins rest and drink. I had told Leo to bring plenty of fluid, and, as I was in the front, I could hear him drinking regularly. What I didn't know was he had a litre bottle of Red Bull.

Night came, and we turned our little head torches on, and we sighted some large lights off to our starboard. Leo thought it was an Oil rig. That Oil rig was heading straight for us, and after some frantic paddling, the shape and lights of the Irish Ferry passed close by us.

We saw the lights of Dun Laorghaire through the dark, but as we paddled on, they never seemed to get closer. Dawn broke, and by this time, the full effects of the Red bull had taken its toll. He had been blathering away most of the night, and now he was falling asleep, and I kept splashing him with water to keep him awake.

We arrived at the ferry port. Leo crawled out of the boat and threw up the remainder of the red bull. We then carried the boat up the breakwater to the loading area and staggered onto the return ferry home.

We snuck the boat back onto the Plas Menai rack and put two cans of Guinness in the cockpits and a postcard from Dublin. A few weeks later, I was working with Alun Williams, head of the centre, and he was regaling me with the story of these two idiots who had kayaked across the Irish sea just missing the ferry. He hadn't looked on the rack or realised that we had Plas Menai stickers all over the Kayak. Finally, after arriving home late on Sunday, we went to work the next day, and Leo

**PADDLING THROUGH THE NIGHT ON THE
IRISH SEA CROSSING**

found he had to run a week's sea kayaking course.

My next Crossing was from Anglesey to the Isle of Man. I decided to do this solo and in a plastic sea kayak. Neither were brilliant options. I left the North coast of Anglesey at 4 am and paddled into the dawn; it was also early in the year and got dark around 5. I would also be pushed east by the tide and then west later with a fast tide to deal with at the end of the trip around the calf of man, the island's southerly tip. This time the VHF Worked, and I could chat with Liverpool coastguard, who during the trip kept the banter going with tales of coffee and biscuits they were having in their friendly, warm office.

The sea fog was in, but I could tell I was heading in the right direction as I could hear the plane flying towards Ronaldsay, the island's airport.

Going for a pee solo is always more awkward as you can't raft up with another kayak to add stability. I would stop and pee into a plastic bottle, then empty. To keep things simple, I left everything hanging out, ready to go. Darkness fell, and I realised the tide pushed me further north towards Douglas, the main port and the ferry lane. I was now flying along with the tide. I felt a surge of energy and rhythm after 14 hours. I radioed the harbour master, and he told me to get a move on as the ferry was coming. I could see its lights catching me up, and I just managed to arrive before it. The harbour master came down, shaking his head and help me carry the boat out and along the quayside past the ferry passengers disembarking. I had my spray deck clipped up to my jacket, and a cold blast of air down below made me realise that I was also exposing myself to the public

**LEAVING ABERDEEN ON A ATTEMPT TO
PADDLE TO RUSSIA**

as I hadn't bothered to put it all away before landing. I flicked the spay deck off, which concealed the offending item, and we walked out of the port gates.

With this fine resume of experience, was I ready for the North Sea Crossing, three days unsupported on one of the shallowest seas around and attempting the first Crossing from Shetland? Who am I kidding? No, I wasn't. I thought it was a terrible idea, and I was scared shitless.

We got dropped off at Aberdeen. The kayaks were on trolleys, and all our gear was inside the boats. We wheeled them onto the ferry. We arrived in Lerwick and persuaded a local to store the boats in his workshop while we sorted out food. After some warm-up paddles, we headed out to the outer skerries as our launchpad for the Crossing. The boats were regular sea kayaks, but we had a hole behind the cockpit where we could put a stopper to clip the vessels together and slump over each other's decks to sleep. It was challenging to fit in and was moral squalor to get any sleep. We waited on the island on an excellent 5-day forecast, but long term, this was not looking good, and after a week, we had to make a decision.

We decided to take a ferry up to northern Norway and try to do it in reverse; I was relieved that it had postponed the Crossing for a while. We got across to Bergan and walked the boats onto the famous Hurtigruten ferry going north. The old postal ferry that now ran up and down the coast, mainly taking tourists. We couldn't afford a cabin but spent the next seven days sleeping on the deck or in the luggage bays. I was awoken one night by an American couple putting their bags on top of

me. I woke up, and the wife told her husband she had found a stowaway, to which I replied I am not a stowaway madam; I have a ticket.

Eventually, we disembarked at Honningsvaer near Nordkapp, Europe's most northerly point. We wheeled the boats off wearing our kayaking gear. It was a gloomy, cold and unimpressive town, which seemed deserted. It was the world cup final, and Leo being a fan, wanted to watch the match.

The deal was no alcohol. We found a bar, parked the kayaks, walked into this dimly lit and empty room still in all our gear, sat down with cokes, and watched the game. 2 hours later, and we were on the water paddling towards Nordkapp in a Force 4 wind and rough seas.

We found an old fishing cabin to sleep in, and the following morning headed around the cliffs of Nordkapp. This time the wind had died, but

with a good swell and sea mist, the place had the atmosphere of a great Viking hall coming in and out of view. These cliffs are where the tourists go, and it has a museum. It's not the most northern point; this is the preserve of a small peninsula and a long hike a few miles further south.

The next few weeks were of isolated paddling, stunning scenery and Puffin mania. I had never seen so many birds circling some of the islands.

We camped mostly. Occasionally we stayed in old fishing huts. We saw a few people, and the Rhythm of expedition life settled in. I made the breakfast, Leo, the evening meal, supplemented by our fishing efforts.

Eventually, we arrived in the small village of Skjervoy. We pulled directly onto a small campsite by the sea. Here we could get a long overdue shower and go into town for a beer.

**LEO AND THE FRENCH
LEGIONARES UNIFORM**

We wandered into town and found a bar, which was quiet with only two other customers, one of which came straight across to us.

Where are you from, and what are you doing here? He asked; he was a big guy with a weather-beaten face that smelt of salty water. We told him our tale, and he broke into a smile and bought us a drink. We were now his guest; his name was Isaac Isaksson, a local fisherman, and we joined him and other friends arriving. Leo was seated next to another man-mountain, and as the drinks flowed, they were chatting and laughing. He had been away for eighteen years and was back visiting family, and I noticed the scars on his massive forearms, which looked like knife scars.

The evening progressed with more oddballs arriving, and by this time, Isaac had his shirt off

**ON THE WAY HOME AFTER THE ENGLISH
CHANNEL CROSSING**

dancing. He was like some massive Silverback Gorilla. I decided it was time to leave. Because it was still light, it didn't seem like the early hours of the morning. Leo and his friend were still drinking and laughing. I told Isaac I was going, and he looked at Leo and told me the reason that his new friend hadn't been back for eighteen years was that he had strangled a man to death with his hand in Tromso, but he slapped me on the back and told me he would take care of Leo!

The next day no sign of Leo, but somebody had put a note on the tent. We have taken Leo, but we will bring him back. The following morning Leo arrived with two carrier bags. He was still pissed, so I put him to bed. One Carrier bag contained beer, which was the last thing he needed, the other a full French Legionnaire's uniform.

Leo sobered up after a long sleep. It transpires he had been on a long journey. Involving long drives for more alcohol a fishing completion, Isaac ultimately presents him with his old Legionaries uniform. We now had to carry this in the boats, and the following day on the water, Leo wanted to say goodbye to Isaac. Not wishing to lose him again for a few days, I told him to keep paddling and shut up.

The final part of the trip was uneventful, and we finished in Tromso, having run out of time. We loaded the boats on the ferry for the long journey back to Newcastle, hoping customs would not find the Isaacs Uniform. So, we wouldn't have to explain this long story, although it would certainly give us some moral authority if we wore it.

COMING OFF THE NEW ROUTE, APTLY
NAMED 'OBSCURED BY CLOUDS'

The windiest
region in the
world

# CHAPTER
## THIRTEEN

# CAPE FAREWELL

# "We had got an Invite to be guests at the Arctic Club dinner in Cambridge in 2014.

Liam and I had been awarded the Arctic Club award for an expedition around Cape Farewell, the southern tip of Greenland. It was a black-tie event, and we had to give a talk in the morning after dinner at The Scot polar institute. Liam wasn't keen, but one of us had to go, so it was down to me.

It was a fantastic evening full of explorers and scientists, all fascinating people. the following day I had to give a lecture at the Scott Polar Research Institute, and I got to the Institute early; and the curator showed me around, and he let me handle Captain Scott's final diaries found with his body in November 1912 by Apsley Cherry-Gerrard who went on to write one of the classic books on polar adventure, The worst journey in the world

The Arctic Club founded in the 1930s, primarily a Cambridge University club; it promoted expeditions to the Arctic and had an illustrious pedigree of members. I was automatically a member for winning the Award, and the subs were a tenner a year. I was keen if this didn't mean I couldn't apply for funding in the future. I asked how many members, and they weren't quite sure because of the members' age group; some were Deceased but still paying the subs!

We had achieved the Award for a trip to paddle around the southern tip of Greenland and attempt new Alpine-style rock routes on the way; although technically below the Arctic circle, they gave us the Award as they thought it an adventurous trip, how right they were. Cape farewell is the windiest region because it receives more wind between 40mph and 80mph than anywhere else on the planet, with long stretches of coastline not easy to land.

I knew Liam from Plas y Brenin, a good paddler and climber and young and keen, he was slightly shambolic in the eyes of other professionals, but I found him easy company with a dry sense of humour. As always, with just two of you on a paddling trip, you feel more exposed to the risk without a third person's extra help.

We had two flights and a couple of helicopter journeys to arrive at Nanortilak from the U.K. On one of the flights, we met a local helicopter pilot involved in search and rescue. We told him of our plans, the Inuit people are very economical in conversation, but his face and mannerisms indicated this was a bad idea. Nils, our local contact, met us, and after a short walk, we got the kayaks out of a container and set up in the local hotel, and

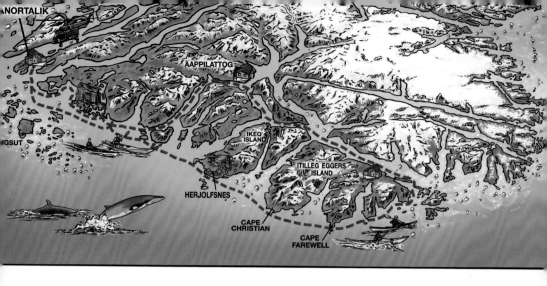

the kayaks put in the old disco. We were the hotels only guests, and we packed the boats in the spooky old disco with the D.J.s cabinet there with all the CDS still in place.

We had arranged to use Glenmore Lodge's kayaks. It was the Scottish national outdoor centre based in Aviemore. Doug, their Head of Canoeing, had rented them to us, but looking at them, I realised how small they were. They were Capella's more suited to week trips, not fitting a month's worth of kit in.

The next day we carried the boats the short distance to the shore and finished the packing. We had 26 days of food camping and climbing kit, and we had kit all over the deck as well. The kayaks were very low in the water as we set off into a stiff breeze and the skeg, a sort of drop keel device to stop the boat from turning into the wind, was ineffective with all the clutter on the deck. A tightly packed into the cockpit with gear, I wouldn't be able to get out very quickly in the event of a capsize.

We had a few days of radio contact with Nils initially, then we would be out of touch and no way to check the weather, so as the forecast looked good, we headed east towards Cape Farewell. We

manage to stash some of the food bags over the next few days to lighten the boats as we return this way. Each pack contained all the food for both of us for a day. We stopped at an ancient Viking settlement called Herjolfsnes and camped. It was strange as this was one of the first landing points for them, the remains of an old church remained, and the weather was eroding the graves. Allowing human remains to spill into the sea, it was a beautiful isolated place and where it all eventually finished for the last settlement.

The following day started foggy as we set off for the Cape, but the winds were light as we passed under the sheer cliffs of Cape Christian. As we came around, the wind picked up, and the cloud cleared, and we could see Cape Farewell in the distance and breaking waves on what I assumed were low lying rocks. I was relying on all my previous experiences to make the right call as we got closer. The possible consequences were too high, and I shouted to Liam to head into the bay between the headlands.

It was t over, yet we now had a sizeable rocky beach to deal with breaking waves and a steep beach angle; luckily, we had plastic sea kayaks, so we had to time the dramatic exit to do minor damage; to ourselves and kit. I came flying up the beach and managed to get out and drag my boat and then help Liam land. I am glad we got out as the wind continued to increase for the rest of the day. We were stuck here for another day, but at last, the wind died, and we headed off into a foggy and atmospheric morning. Convinced the wind was going to pick up, we rounded the Cape with the mist slowly clearing. It was the crux of the trip, and in my relief, I got caught unawares by an extensive set of swell and almost got trashed; I paddled away to see Liam grinning,' I knew you'd be okay, 'he said.

The Cape was the crux of the trip, and it was good to get it behind us; the weather improved, almost a sign that we were over the worst bit. We found a campsite near some climbing potential and spent the next few days climbing some new routes. We were now in the shelter of the fjord system, with stunning scenery, but we still had to cross open stretches of water, and with the sun out, we often paddled with our drysuits undone. The wind picked up on one crossing from a gentle breeze to strong wind and rolling waves, but we couldn't stop to do our dry suits up, and the thought of going in the water or rolling was out of the question, so it was with relief we reached the other side.

We camped on a very exposed rocky headland, and the wind continued to increase, but we found one large boulder that we managed to tuck in behind while the wind blew for another day; stuck in the tent we read and slept and on one occasion, we looked out to see a minke whale go past. We had already had one encounter where it had come straight for us, diving at the last moment.

There was one small settlement of 60 people, and we stopped here and picked up a couple of things at the little store. An official from Nuuk, the capital about 400 km north, was here for a few

weeks sorting out local administration. She sorts of latched onto us when she saw us; she had had a minimal conversation with locals and was getting desperate for company. She cooked us a lovely lunch while Liam was in the bathroom. I asked her the meat in the dish; she said Polar bear. Shot around the village a few weeks ago. This time we didn't have a gun as everybody said; it's too far south for bears; after my previous encounter, I should have ignored their advice. I never told Liam, so both of us worried, but I had a couple of restless nights in the tent.

We carried on down the fjords for the next week and eventually found an abandoned house near some possible climbing objective. The next day we started climbing. It was a long day, the usual mix of mountain rock, route finding and good climbing. The good thing was that it doesn't get dark in the summer months, so we just carried on climbing till we reached the top; the cloud was rolling off the mountains like a cup of frothy milk poured from a large cup, and the sea shimmered as we began our descent.

The weather changed after this, getting colder, and it snowed high up. We were stranded in the spooky old house for a few days, with the former inhabitants' graves just over a slight rise. We were on our way back now picking up some of the food stashes we had left on the way out; remarkably, they were all in one piece.

One of the last camps was in a sheltered bay, and that morning, we had to decide if we were going to leave to head out on the open sea. It looked okay from our restricted vantage point, and we headed out. We were now committed, on an exposed steep coast with icebergs, the wind picked up, and with

some tide, the seas started to increase, breaking tops. With nowhere to run except to keep going to, we reached the next bay; I got the occasional glimpse of Liam through the swell and gripped all my body stiff. My skill level dropping, short strokes, with capsizing, not an option, it was one of the scariest seas I had been in, we were a small craft in a tremendous unforgiving environment, and we had made a poor decision.

At last, we rounded the cliffs into the bay, but now we had to deal with a side wind, although at least we would be washed up onto a more forgiving coast if we had a problem. We landed exhausted but intact, and we got into our routine, tent up, change of clothes, brew on the gas stove and then off to find firewood.

The wind continued to blow, but eventually, we managed to get the last stretch back into

Nanortilak done. We pulled the boats up, unloaded them, and Nils put us in a lovely hut near the sea.

Liam wanted to go out to a local bar, and I warned him that the locals like a drink and could get very persistent. After an hour of harassment, not in a wrong way, but by people with raised voices saying he smelt terrible, he had had enough, and we went home to the quiet of our little hut.

We had a few days left, and the following day a large Cruiseship arrived. A few stop every year and the village swamped with tourists with cameras. The locals mostly hid away, feeling like animals in a Zoo. We helped Nils in the tourist shop, and he said the locals accepted us and were surprised we had managed to return okay. Kayaking in Boats similar to what their ancestors used for hunting, but now we're only faded pictures or relics in their small museum in the town.

# OLLY
# **SANDERS**

Nominated for the Piolet D'Or in 2003 for a first ascent in Alaska and awarded the Arctic Club Award twice for remote journies in Arctic regions. Olly has climbed worldwide, big walling, alpine ascents in the Himalayas, emphasising small teams and self-reliance. A mix of success, but many failures, especially in the high mountains. Combining sea kayaking and climbing to access remote areas. The focus has been on having a good time with friends with humour at its centre.

He has worked in the outdoors industry for 30 years, achieving the top UK awards in mountaineering and kayaking. He has produced instructional DVDs in both aspects.

He worked as an arena rigger and Stunt rigger in a previous life. He has toured with Genesis, Rolling Stones, Michael Jackson, Paul McCartney, and worked on some Batman movies.